MARYJANE'S
STITCHING ROOM

MARYJANE'S
STITCHING ROOM

BY

MaryJane Butters

PHOTOGRAPHS BY

MaryJane Butters & Erik Jacobson

CLARKSON POTTER/PUBLISHERS
NEW YORK

Published in the United States by Clarkson Potter/Publishers, an imprint of the Crown Publishing Group, a division of Random House, Inc., New York.
www.crownpublishing.com
www.clarksonpotter.com

Library of Congress Cataloging-in-Publication Data

Butters, MaryJane, 1953–
MaryJane's Stitching Room / by MaryJane Butters ; photographs by MaryJane Butters and Erik Jacobson.—1st ed.
p. cm.
1. Needlework—Patterns. 2. Home economics. I. Title.
TT753.B93 2007
746.4041—dc22

2006038177

ISBN 978-1-4000-8048-9

Printed in the United States of America

10 9 8 7 6 5 4 3 2 1

First Edition

Art Direction by MaryJane Butters and Carol Hill
Design by Carol Hill

All of us at MaryJanesFarm welcome your comments and suggestions. Write to us at iris@maryjanesfarm.org or visit us on the Web at www.maryjanesfarm.org.

AUTHOR'S NOTE

Hey farmgirl friend, welcome! Let's start by pretending you're here with me at my farm. Imagine the chickens cackling (braggin' about another egg laid), and a rooster telling us it's still morning. Then picture my pregnant Jersey milk cow, Chocolate, looking up, thinking you've brought her a treat—something oat-y with a hint of molasses. (Chocolate loves molasses so much that I'm flirtin' with naming her baby Mo if it's a boy and Lass if it's a girl!) She turns a circle, kicks up her hind legs, and comes a runnin' (she loves to lick my cheek when I pamper her). Adorable! I know you're nobody's fool, but cow breath, all warm and sweet, is the ultimate best, like fresh-mowed hay. After you and I grab a hug from each other, we'll wander through the rooms of my house; but first, let's put some water on for tea and head for the table and chairs by the window that are flooded in the morning sun ...

“It is a token of healthy and gentle characteristics when women of high thoughts and accomplishments love to sew; especially as they are never more at home with their own hearts than while so occupied.”
– Nathaniel Hawthorne

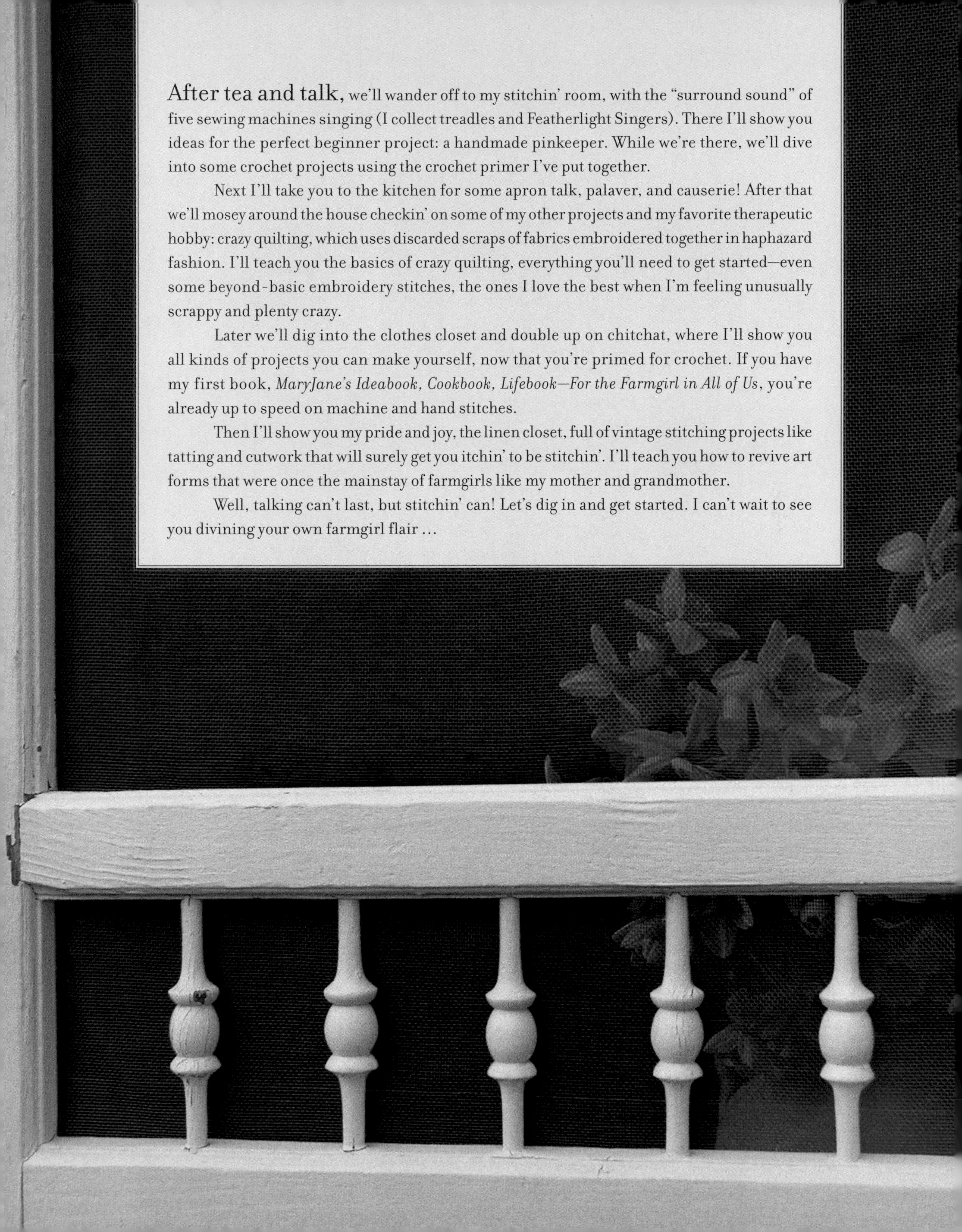

After tea and talk, we'll wander off to my stitchin' room, with the "surround sound" of five sewing machines singing (I collect treadles and Featherlight Singers). There I'll show you ideas for the perfect beginner project: a handmade pinkeeper. While we're there, we'll dive into some crochet projects using the crochet primer I've put together.

Next I'll take you to the kitchen for some apron talk, palaver, and causerie! After that we'll mosey around the house checkin' on some of my other projects and my favorite therapeutic hobby: crazy quilting, which uses discarded scraps of fabrics embroidered together in haphazard fashion. I'll teach you the basics of crazy quilting, everything you'll need to get started—even some beyond-basic embroidery stitches, the ones I love the best when I'm feeling unusually scrappy and plenty crazy.

Later we'll dig into the clothes closet and double up on chitchat, where I'll show you all kinds of projects you can make yourself, now that you're primed for crochet. If you have my first book, *MaryJane's Ideabook, Cookbook, Lifebook—For the Farmgirl in All of Us*, you're already up to speed on machine and hand stitches.

Then I'll show you my pride and joy, the linen closet, full of vintage stitching projects like tatting and cutwork that will surely get you itchin' to be stitchin'. I'll teach you how to revive art forms that were once the mainstay of farmgirls like my mother and grandmother.

Well, talking can't last, but stitchin' can! Let's dig in and get started. I can't wait to see you divining your own farmgirl flair …

CONTENTS

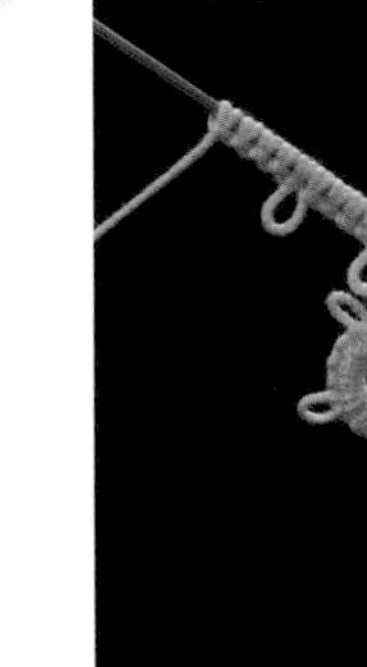

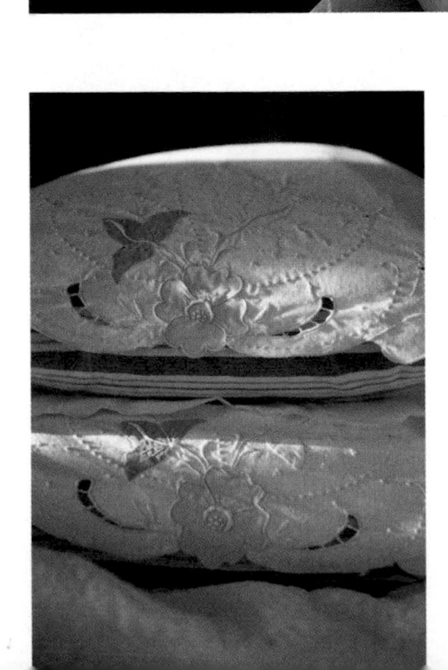

DEDICATION

This book is dedicated to the miracle in my life, my mother . . .

In her hands, I've been nurtured.
Always loved.
My hands are her work, this work.

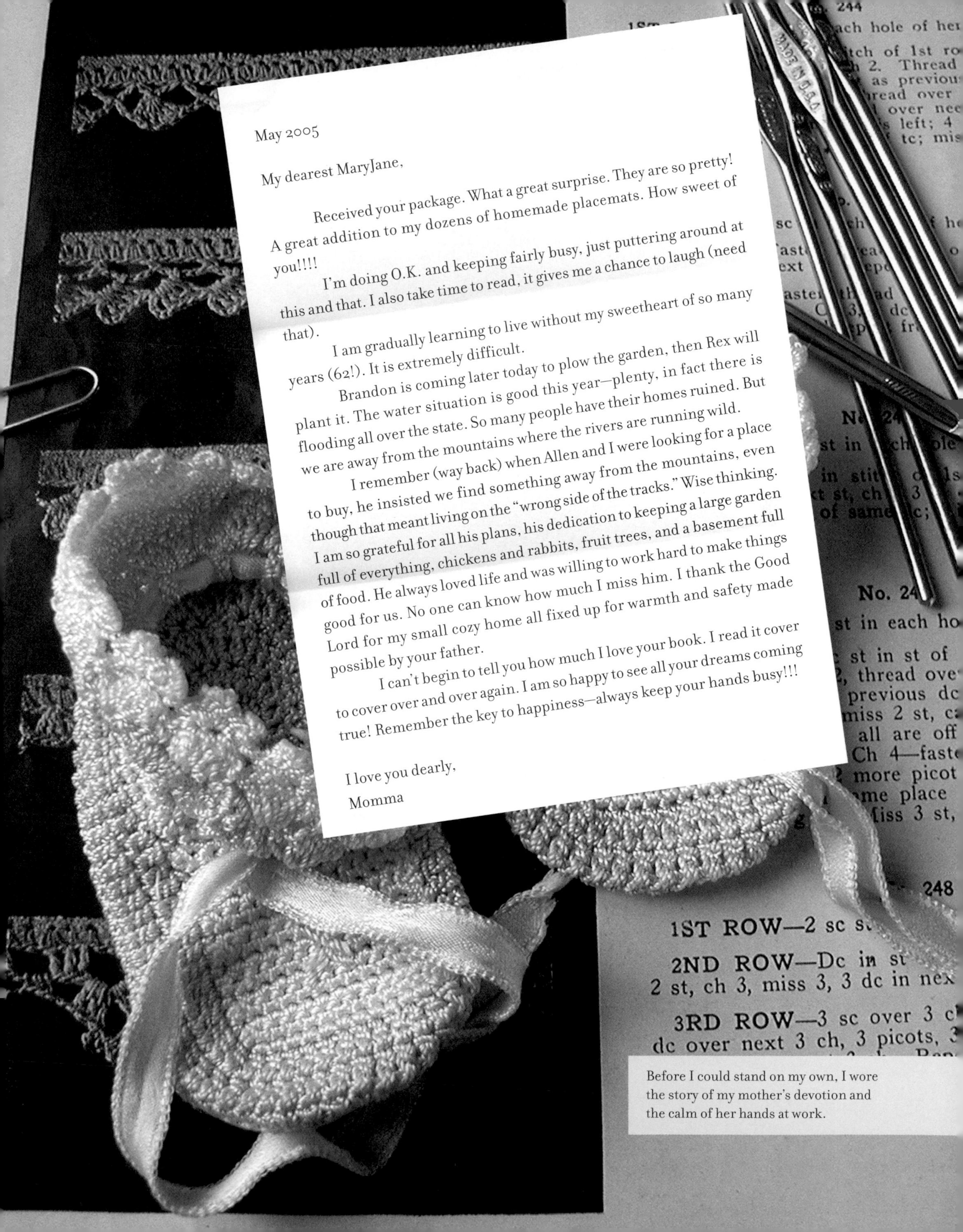

May 2005

My dearest MaryJane,

Received your package. What a great surprise. They are so pretty! A great addition to my dozens of homemade placemats. How sweet of you!!!!

I'm doing O.K. and keeping fairly busy, just puttering around at this and that. I also take time to read, it gives me a chance to laugh (need that).

I am gradually learning to live without my sweetheart of so many years (62!). It is extremely difficult.

Brandon is coming later today to plow the garden, then Rex will plant it. The water situation is good this year—plenty, in fact there is flooding all over the state. So many people have their homes ruined. But we are away from the mountains where the rivers are running wild.

I remember (way back) when Allen and I were looking for a place to buy, he insisted we find something away from the mountains, even though that meant living on the "wrong side of the tracks." Wise thinking. I am so grateful for all his plans, his dedication to keeping a large garden full of everything, chickens and rabbits, fruit trees, and a basement full of food. He always loved life and was willing to work hard to make things good for us. No one can know how much I miss him. I thank the Good Lord for my small cozy home all fixed up for warmth and safety made possible by your father.

I can't begin to tell you how much I love your book. I read it cover to cover over and over again. I am so happy to see all your dreams coming true! Remember the key to happiness—always keep your hands busy!!!

I love you dearly,

Momma

Before I could stand on my own, I wore the story of my mother's devotion and the calm of her hands at work.

GETTING STARTED *Stitching*

I'd like you to think of this first *Stitching Room* workbook as your crochet and tatting primer and the book you go to when you feel some basic embroidery or cutwork coming on. I've tossed in plenty of handiwork projects, all of them budget minded. Not only did we design and create all the patterns in this book here at my farm, we modeled, photographed, and illustrated them as well—nimble with thimbles we are!

Because I believe that creating a signature pinkeeper is the perfect starting place for a life well sewn, I've included ideas for making pinkeepers using beginner hand stitches that won't even require a trip to town, since they're made using common discards, scraps of fabric, glue, and things like jelly jars, old gelatin molds, cast-iron patty molds, and spools.

And given that "farmgirl is a condition of the heart," you'll find directions for a heart-shaped pinkeeper that can be made from any fabric you have on hand. I like creating new hearts from old worn-out quilts. Once you decide to take up crochet (I do think our projects are irresistible), you can honor our Victorian foremothers by dressing up your heart in a delicate, show-off crochet cover like the ones at right.

Creating a Signature *Pinkeeper*

"'Tis a gift to be simple, 'Tis a gift to be free,
'Tis a gift to come down where you ought to be."

– Shaker hymn

I make simple pinkeepers like this one and those on the following pages by simply gathering material around my chosen stuffing (see tips at right), tying the ball at the bottom with string or a rubber band, trimming, and gluing the ball into an old cast-iron patty mold, canning jar, or gelatin mold.

Jelly Jar *Pinkeeper*

Supply List

1 scrap fabric, about 12" x 12"
1 1/2-pint jelly jar, without lid
40 small scraps of fabric in varying colors, about 4" x 4"
1 skein black embroidery floss
1 spool all-purpose sewing thread
Embroidery needle
Stuffing

Instructions

1. Lay the large scrap of fabric on your work surface, right side down. Set the jelly jar in the middle of it, top up. Pick up the edges of the fabric and pull them up to enclose the jar. Gather them together across the mouth of the jar, pin the fabric in place, and stitch securely.
2. Place one of the small scraps of fabric facedown on your work surface. Place your chosen stuffing in the center of it. Gather up the edges of the fabric to enclose the stuffing, creating a fabric "stem." Push a threaded needle through the stem and wrap the thread around it several times. Secure with a knot. Repeat with the remaining scraps of fabric.
3. Embellish the center of each ball with a French knot (page 52).
4. Working on the back side of the balls (the side where the fabric is gathered and held in place), make a patchwork of balls by stitching them together in a circular shape (refer to photo at right).
5. Place a few uncovered balls of stuffing on top of the fabric that is covering the top of the jelly jar to create a dome shape. Place the patchwork of balls on top, making sure the outermost balls overlap the edge of the jar. Stitch your patchwork of balls to the fabric that is covering the jelly jar to complete your pinkeeper.

Stuffing It

Common cotton balls will work, but only if you pull them apart and fluff them first. Otherwise, poly stuffing is ideal; the needles seem to meet with less resistance. Or use fine sand (you might need a thin liner) and dried lavender—a sachet and pinkeeper rolled into one. The sand will help keep your needles sharp. Better yet, try sawdust. (I took apart a store-bought pinkeeper that worked well and found plain sawdust inside.) If you have a local source for raw wool (washed, of course, so it doesn't create oily lanolin stains on your fabric), it is as fluffy as poly stuffing and doesn't shift around like cotton. Family haircuts? Don't toss your locks ... they also make excellent stuffing; likewise, old panty hose.

Know someone itchin' to get stitchin'...

or striking out on their own? A beginner's pinkeeper is easy to make using any size canning jar you can find. Fill it with extra buttons for mending, a tape measure, a small pair of scissors, three small spools of mending thread (black, white, and tan), a thimble, and a few safety pins. Top it off with a ball of stuffing encased in a scrap of fabric that is then wrapped around the inner lid and stitched. Adorn it with pins and needles.

Using the idea on the previous page, cover your fabric ball with a pretty doily before gluing it in place like the gelatin-mold pinkeeper at bottom left.
Over time, I've discovered that knick-knacks can become pinkeepers too!

What's Project F.A.R.M.? F.A.R.M. stands for First-class American Rural Made, and it's a project that was conceived here, at my farm. As rural communities fade and farmers continue to disappear from our landscape, we decided something must be done to support those struggling to maintain their rural lifestyle. That's where Project F.A.R.M. comes in.

Rural America is full of unsung crafters—hardworking men and women, young and old, who deserve their fair share and find it hard, if not impossible, to compete in today's marketplace. To that end, many of the products we sell on our website or in stores "come with a face"—you can "meet" or "get to know" the person behind the product. As the concept grows and you see our Project F.A.R.M. label on more and more products nationwide, you'll be able to support rural people like Miss Wilma and Friends of Kentucky (Wilma made this needle "sewie thang" and boasts she has burned up seven sewing machines making pillows for us) and the women of rural Idaho who sew our "Farmgirl at Heart" tote bags.

Buying something made by hand from someone you "know" is our concept of how the world should be, and once was not so very long ago. To find out more, go to our website, www.maryjanesfarm.org.

CROCHETED *Pinkeeper*

Now that you've gifted all your friends with easy-to-make pinkeepers, you're ready to create a vintage-style crocheted pinkeeper. This project makes a cover for the 4 1/2" quilted heart pillow at right. First, you'll crochet the back of the cover (see photo, top left) using our crochet primer starting on page 118, then you'll crochet the front edge or ruffle (see photo, bottom left).

Supply List

1 ball no. 8 cotton perle crochet thread
1 4 1/2" quilted heart pillow (instructions on page 21)
Size 10 (1.25 mm) steel crochet hook

Gauge: Rows 1–32 = 3" x 4 1/4"

Instructions

Back

Starting at top, ch 12.
Row 1: Sc in second ch from hook, sc in each of next 5-ch, ch 3, sc in same ch as last sc, sc in each of the next 5-ch. Ch 1, turn.
Rows 2–11: 2 sc in first sc (an increase), sc in each sc across up to ch-3 sp, in ch-3 sp make sc, ch 3, sc, sc in each sc across until last sc, 2 sc in last sc (another increase). Ch 1, turn.
Row 12: Same as Row 11, but omit increases at both ends. Ch 1, turn.
Row 13: Same as Row 11.
Rows 14–21: Repeat Row 12 and Row 13 alternately.
Rows 22–27: Same as Row 12, but decrease (dec) 1 sc at both ends of row (to dec 1 sc, start off on the second st from hook). Ch 1, turn.
Rows 28–32: Same as Row 27, but dec 2 sc (start on third st from hook) at both ends of each row.

Hereafter, work is done in rounds instead of rows, as follows:
Rnd 1: Sc closely together around to ch-3 sp, sl st in sp.
Rnd 2: Ch 5 (to count as dc and ch 2), dc in sp, *ch 2, skip 1 sc, dc in next sc. Repeat from * around, ending rnd with ch, sl st in third st of ch-5 first made.
Rnd 3: 3 sc in each sp around. Join with sl st.
Rnd 4: Sc in each sc around. Join with sl st.
Rnd 5: Ch 7 (to count as tr and ch 2), *skip 1 sc, tr in next sc, ch 4. Repeat from * to within 5 sc from center top sc, ch 4, skip 1 sc, tr in next sc, skip 1 sc, dc in next sc, skip 1 sc, sc in center top sc (thus completing half of rnd). Work other half of rnd to correspond, joining last ch 4 with sl st to fourth st of ch-7 first made.
Rnd 6: *Sc in next sp, in next sp make 5 dc with ch-1 between each dc, sc in next sp (1 shell made). Repeat from * around. Join with sl st. Fasten off.

Just learnin' to crochet or need a refresher?

See my crochet primer—everything from positioning your hands, to basic and more complicated stitches, to attaching pieces together—complete with both photos and drawings, starting on page 118.

Front

Attach thread to any sc between dcs (on first row of spaces).

Rnd 1: Ch 5 (to count as dc and ch 2), *dc in sc between next 2 dcs, ch 2. Repeat from * around, joining last ch 2 with sl st to third st of ch-5 first made.

Rnd 2 & 3: Sl st to center of first sp, ch 4 (to count as dc and ch 1), *dc in next sp, ch 1. Repeat from * around. Join.

Rnd 4: Ch 3, dc in each sp around. Join.

Rnd 5: *Ch 5, sk 2 dc, sc in next dc. Repeat from * around. Fasten off.

To finish, make a chain about 12 inches long for a pull cord, and weave it in and out through the loops of your last row of crochet. Insert your cushion, pull the chain tight, and tie in a bow or wrap it around a button sewn on the front.

Quilt-Scraps Heart

1. Make a pattern by folding a piece of paper in half and drawing half a heart; cut out (remember to make your pattern slightly larger than the size you want your heart to be to allow for seams).
2. Using the pattern, cut two pieces from an old, worn-out quilt.
3. With right sides together, pin and machine stitch around the heart using a 1/2" seam allowance, leaving a 1" gap on one side to allow for filling.
4. Clip curves so the finished piece will lie flat, being careful not to cut through stitches.
5. Turn the pinkeeper right side out and fill it with stuffing (see page 15).
6. Close seam with a whip stitch.

Quilt-Scraps "Jo Jacket"

If we all sipped our morning coffee from a reusable travel mug for one week, we'd save enough trees to fill two football fields. One day, and we'd save a thousand gallons of gasoline. I don't always travel with a mug, but I do keep a reusable Jo Jacket in my purse. I know, it only helps a tiny bit, but I'm also drinking in the warmth of a lovingly handmade quilt.

Enlarge the pattern below by 200 percent. Select an intact piece of an old, worn-out quilt, and fold it in half, right sides together. Place the pattern on top of the fabric, and cut it out. With the fabric still folded, stitch a 5/8" seam along the short edge. Finish the top and bottom edges using bias tape. Dress up your jacket with some buttons.

BoYs who CRoCHet

In a home for troubled kids, a teenage boy named Tom cries out in the middle of an outburst of uncontrolled anger, "Patsy, tell them how good I am when I'm crocheting!"

Patsy, the teacher assistant, asks to have some time alone with Tom. She gives him his crochet hook and lap quilt. Tom crochets for two full hours without stopping. Afterward he is calm.

At the Northwest Children's Home in Lewiston, Idaho, scenes like this, where troubled boys find healing through crochet, are an everyday occurrence.

These are not kids who are at risk because they stayed out too late a few times; they are boys who have suffered abuse in their families so severe it drew the attention of Child Protection Services. Many are former drug addicts. These are kids filled with unmanageable anger and anxiety. After their families failed them, after foster care failed them, after being referred by a court order or a service agency, the Northwest Children's Home welcomed them.

Needlework is strong medicine for anyone, but for these young men it helps rebuild their very core. On a typical Friday in a NCH classroom, ten boys can be found calmly crocheting together in silence. They are focused on their hands, which move in a steady rhythm as they loop and pull, loop and pull.

Several boys are wearing crocheted slippers they made in class. In addition, the boys have filled a box with lap quilts they plan on donating to a local retirement home. Some are purple, others pale green, gray mixed with tan and purple, and pure white.

Each boy chose the materials for his quilt from a box of donated yarns. One boy made a lap quilt in three stripes that match the Mexican flag. Another boy, with his head shaved except for a ring of hair at the top, chose soft hues for his first quilt: pale yellow, pink, white, and pale blue. His next quilt will be pure white like those given to infants for christenings.

As they crochet, the boys learn patience. They trade stories about unraveling row after row of knotted yarn because things weren't right. One boy proudly states he had to rip his slippers out five times before he finally got it right.

"When I'm crocheting, I'm not in trouble," one boy says.

Another confides, "It helps keep me under control."

What is it about crochet that helps me relax and tackle the concerns in my mind at the same time? Perhaps it's the repetition of creating stitches. Or is it because I now expect to relax when I crochet? Maybe it's because I simply love to crochet. It's all of these things and something more. I've made something! Regardless of my mood and thoughts or the crush of the world around me, I have created fabric. I can choose to rip out the stitches and start again, or turn it into something useful and hardworking, or something decorative and elegant. The power is mine ... That just might be the most healing part of crochet. It was made by your own two hands, the loops of yarn combine in stitches to compose fabric under your fingertips. In your hands it feels just right. It feels like peace.

– Cecily Keim
www.SuchSweetHands.com

"It helps me think about what I'm doing, forcing me to calm down and get control of my anger."

Another boy speaks in very fast, clipped sentences that tumble one onto another. "I don't worry about stuff when I crochet ... I don't worry about my grandma ... my grandma died ... my dad is upset ... I didn't know my grandma ... I felt bad for my dad ... I don't worry about my dad when I crochet."

Initially the boys resisted crochet. Sam, a boy who wears a sweatshirt with flames on the sleeves, vowed, "I'm not learning to crochet. Do you think I'm a girl?" Another said, "Crocheting is stupid. It's for geeks." But now these boys know their crochet, and one boy demonstrates the difference between a single crochet, a double crochet, and a shell.

As the boys file out for lunch, Patsy mentions that crocheting also helps with addictions. Keeping their hands busy has helped some boys work through cravings for drugs or alcohol. She said the boys who have addiction problems are often the ones who take to crocheting the quickest.

She believes that crocheting has helped the boys with their anger because it is a calming motion, like rocking a baby or rocking in a chair. It has also been helpful for boys with anxiety problems. Some are so anxious that their hands shake constantly; when they crochet, their hands don't shake.

Patsy has also taught the boys how to sew on buttons and mend clothes. They've learned cake decorating, and now they decorate a cake for each boy who leaves. They've also done cooking projects and learned how to do their own laundry.

These boys want to heal. With crocheting, everyday counseling, and lots of love from the staff, the boys have a chance to rebuild their lives, one stitch at a time.

If you have leftover yarn, the boys would appreciate receiving it at:

Northwest Children's Home
P.O. Box 1288
Lewiston, Idaho 83501

For more information about crocheting as a tool for healing, or to support this important program, contact Patsy Gottschalk, 208-746-1601 ext. 270.

KITCHEN *Stitchin'*

Fancy Work *Apron*

Supply List

1 1/8 yards 45"-wide fabric, washed
3 1/2 yards 1/2"-wide bias tape, washed
2 3/4 yards medium rickrack, washed
1 scrap fabric 7" square to match bias tape for pocket, washed
1 spool all-purpose sewing thread

Assembling, Stitching, and Finishing Details

(5/8" seam allowance unless otherwise indicated)

Bottom Ruffle and Apron Skirt

1. Fold the bottom ruffle in half lengthwise and press. This crease will be your guide for sewing the rickrack. Align rickrack on the right side of fabric so the middle falls over the crease, and stitch down the center of the rickrack.
2. Turn one long edge of the ruffle under 1/4" twice and press. Stitch to hem.
3. Gather the other long edge of the bottom ruffle to fit the bottom curved edge of the apron skirt piece. Stitch with right sides together.
4. On the right side of the apron, center rickrack over the seam you just made and stitch down the middle of the rickrack to attach to apron.

Pocket

Use the scrap of fabric that is the same color as your bias tape for the pocket. Turn under 1/4" on all four sides of the pocket and press. Turn an additional 1/4" at the top of the pocket, press and topstitch. Appliqué or embroider something onto the pocket, as shown at right, if you wish. Pin pocket to apron where shown on pattern, and topstitch sides and bottom 1/8" from pocket edge. Alternately, you can use the same material as your apron body and trim the side and bottom edges of the pocket with rickrack so the middle of the rickrack (where you will stitch to apron skirt) is over the stitching. Stitch in place.

Waistband, Neck Strap, and Apron Bib

1. Gather the top of the apron skirt to fit one long edge of the waistband. With right sides together, stitch.
2. Sew back of neck strap pieces together with a French seam where indicated on pattern.
3. Trim the inside edge of neck strap with bias tape.
4. Place apron bib wrong side up on surface. Place the neck strap, wrong side down, on top of the apron bib, matching notches. Pin bias tape in place on top edge of apron bib, covering both the top edge of apron bib and bottom edge of neck straps. Stitch close to inside edge of bias tape.

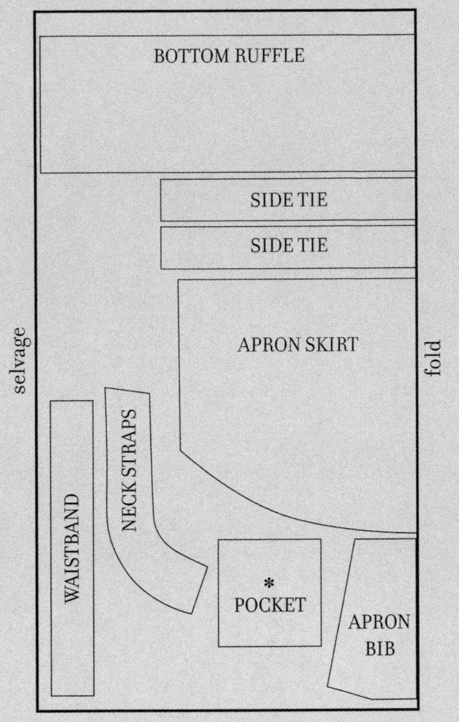

CUTTING DIAGRAM
(*Do not cut this piece if using scrap of coordinating material for pocket.)
If using a one-way print, reorient pattern pieces to match print.

If the fabric you're using has a fun detail like a flower or a vegetable, cut a couple of them out and appliqué them onto the pocket (see page 33), then finish with a decorative blanket stitch (see page 52).

5. Pin bias tape in place along sides of apron bib and outside curve of neck strap. Do not pin along bottom of apron bib. Stitch in place.

Finishing

Place apron skirt on surface wrong side up. Match the center of the unfinished bottom edge of apron bib with the center of the top of the apron skirt and place on top of skirt, right side up. Place side ties on top of apron skirt (right side up), matching notches. Pin bias tape in place all the way up one side of apron, across the waist where the apron meets the bib, and down the other side. Stitch in place. Open out apron bib and topstitch upper edge of bias tape to apron bib to secure.

Make copies of these pages; then enlarge them 400 percent for your life-size MaryJanesFarm pattern.

fold

SIDE TIES
(Cut 2)

fold

BOTTOM RUFFLE
(Cut 1)

Note: You'll only need one notch on each piece. Since tie is cut on fold, you'll have two—only mark a notch at one end.

"In America, in a tenement flat, my grandmother wore one apron and over it another, to keep the first one clean for when company came."

— E. Shakir, Lebanese author and professor

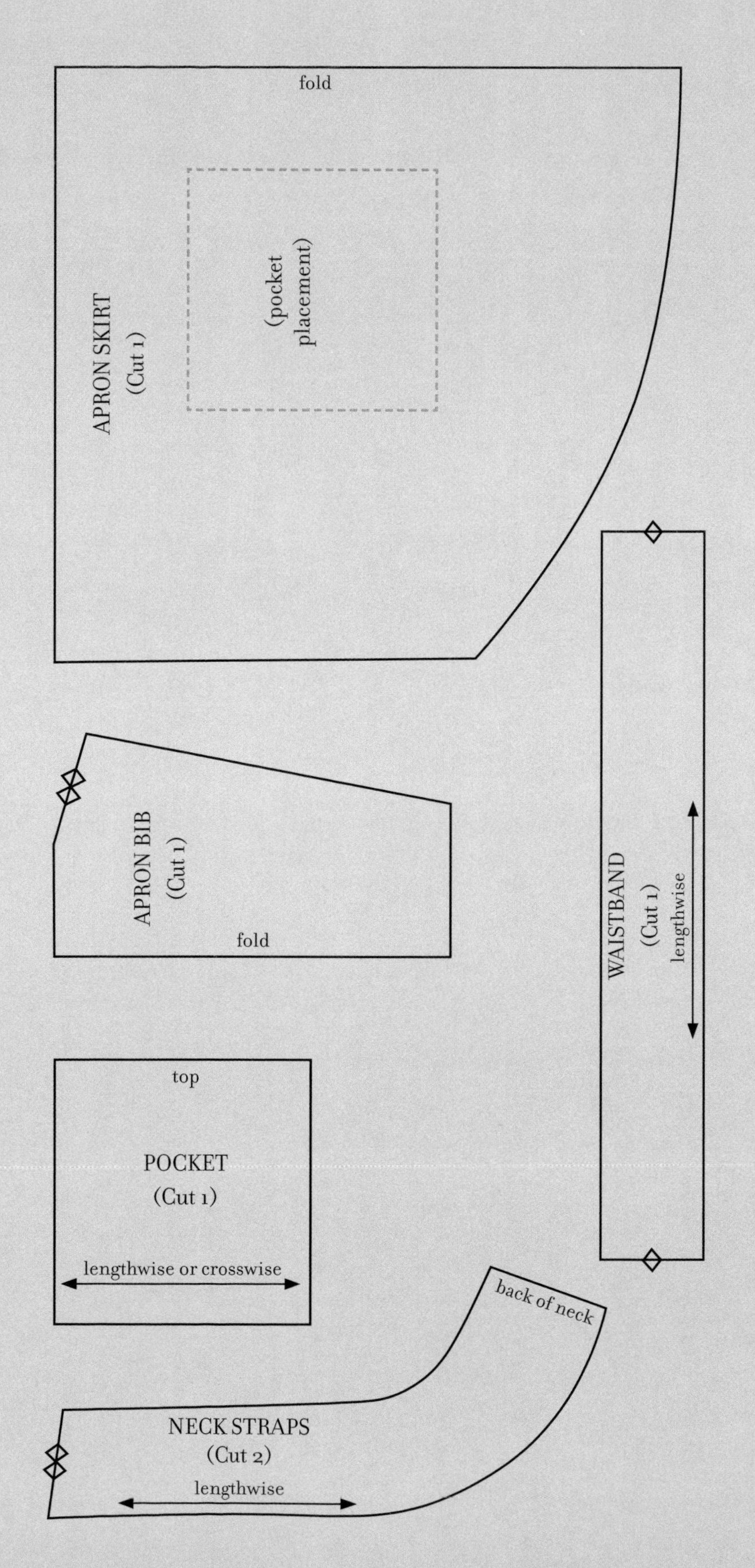

The Button Box

The shades are drawn, the lamps are lit
Across the walls vague shadows flit.
And Mother, smiling, gently rocks
And dreams above her button box.

The button box, the button box,
With souvenirs of vanished frocks
And party gowns of yesteryear,
Old fashioned now, but once how dear.

These disks of metal, bone and shell
Have each a little tale to tell;
And that which keeps the varied hoard—
The battered box—so richly stored,
To her who loves remembrance, is
A treasury of memories.

That giant button had its day
On Father's ulster, rough and gray—
A shield of horn that Baby John
So loved to try his teeth upon;
While this, that might have served an elf,
Belonged to Baby John himself.
That pearly whiteness held in place
Some part of Edith's bridal lace;
And this appeared on nothing less
Than Mary's graduation dress.

These sparkling bits of glass recall
A Christmas feast, a New Year's ball;
And who that saw her could forget
When grandma wore these rounds of jet.

And, oh, what memories of pride,
Of dread, of hope and joy abide
In this bronze button beloved the best,
Whereon the eagle seal is pressed,
That gleamed through flame and battle
storm
Upon a khaki uniform!

The button box of long ago!
Its true delights the children know
Who thread its many colored gems
For necklaces and diadems;
Or in their vivid play behold,
A pirate chest of pearls and gold!
And this worn coffer they who will
May find a fairy casket still,
When Memory her stores unlocks
And pours them from her button box.

–Arthur Guiterman

VARIATION: FANCY WORK *Apron* WITH WAIST RUFFLE

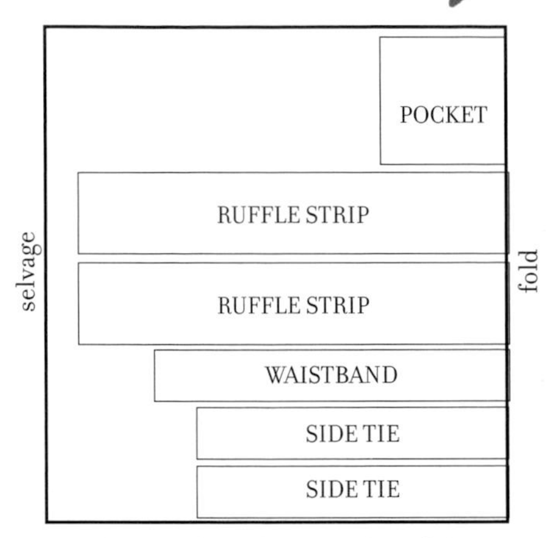

CUTTING DIAGRAM: FABRIC B

Supply List

1/2	yard 45"-wide fabric A (large floral in photo), washed
2/3	yard 45"-wide fabric B (small print in photo), washed
1/4	yard 45"-wide fabric C (geometic print in photo), washed
1	spool all-purpose sewing thread

Cutting

(*pattern pieces from Fancy Work Apron on previous pages)

Fabric A: Cut out the apron skirt*.
Fabric B: Cut out the pocket*, waistband*, side ties*, and 2 strips 4" x 42" for bottom ruffle (see cutting diagram above).
Fabric C: Cut 1 strip 1 3/4" x 42" for center of bottom ruffle, 2 strips 1 1/2" x 42" for lower edge of bottom ruffle, and 1 strip 1 1/2" x 34" for waist ruffle.

Assembling, Stitching, and Finishing Details

(1/4" seam allowance unless otherwise indicated)

Apron Skirt and Bottom Ruffle

1. The 1 3/4" x 42" strip from Fabric C will be the center piece of your bottom ruffle. With right sides together, take one strip from Fabric B and sew it to one long side of the center piece. Sew the second strip from Fabric B to the other long side of the center piece. Press seams open. Turn under the bottom edge 1/4"; press. At the top edge, stitch a gathering row (long, loose stitches with ends long enough to pull) 1/8" from the raw edge.
2. With right sides together and matching centers and side edges, pin bottom ruffle to apron skirt. Adjust gathers to fit and stitch. Press seam toward apron skirt.
3. Turn under sides of apron 1/4" twice and press. Stitch to hem.

Pocket

Turn under 1/4" on all four sides of the pocket and press. Turn an additional 1/4" at the top of the pocket, press and topstitch. Pin pocket to apron according to pocket placement on pattern and topstitch sides and bottom 1/8" from pocket edge.

Waistband and Side Ties

With right sides together, sew the side ties to the waistband at the sides, matching notches. At the top of the apron skirt, sew a gathering row 1/8" from the edge. With the right side of the waistband along the wrong side of the apron skirt, pin, with raw edges even, matching centers, and adjusting gathers to fit waistband. Stitch a 1/4" seam. Turn under 1/4" all around the remaining edges; press. Fold the waistband and ties in half lengthwise, wrong sides together, and press. Turn apron to right side.

Waistband Ruffle

Take the 1 3/4" x 34" strip of Fabric C and turn under one long edge and both ends 1/4" twice, press, and stitch. Sew a gathering row 1/8" from edge along other long edge of ruffle. Place ruffle right side out on top of apron at waistband, matching raw edges and adjusting gathers to fit waistband. Fold waistband over, covering gathering row, and pin waistband in place. Pin remaining open long edge and ends of ties together and topstitch, starting at short end of one tie, going along lower edge of tie, waistband, and other tie, and up other short end of tie.

Lower Edge Ruffle

Take the two 1 1/2" x 42" strips of Fabric C and stitch together to form one long piece. Turn under one long edge and both ends 1/4" twice, press and stitch. Sew a gathering row 1/8" from edge along the other long edge of ruffle. Pin ruffle, right side out, along the underside of the lower edge of apron, easing gathers to fit, and topstitch in place.

"I sort of fell asleep that day
While milking that old cow
My head was nestled in her flank
I still can feel it now."

— Otto Rosfeld

You can print two more variations of our Fancy Work Apron from my website: www.maryjanesfarm.org/StitchingRoom. Also, check out the Fancy Work Apron Libbie (at right) is wearing on page 97.

Daffodil Table Runner

Supply List

Slightly coarse linen-y fabric approximately 13" wide by the length you desire, depending on your table
Green, light yellow, and dark yellow fabric for appliquéd leaves and flowers, less than 1/8 yard of each
Black, green, gold, and light yellow embroidery floss, one skein each
Red wax transfer pencil
Tracing paper
Embroidery needle
All-purpose sewing thread

Instructions

1. Fold under the edges of your table runner 1/4" twice and press. To hem, stitch close to the inner folded edge on all four sides.
2. Make a copy of the pattern on the facing page; then enlarge it 200 percent for your life-size MaryJanesFarm pattern. Trace the design with a wax pencil onto tracing paper. The daffodil pattern goes at both ends of your runner, connected in between by a long simple row of outline stitches along both long edges of the runner. Transfer the pattern to both ends of your runner on the right side of the fabric by laying the tracing paper upside down on the fabric and ironing it, using the wool setting (no steam). You can pin straight through the paper and fabric into your ironing board to keep the transfer from sliding around. Try not to wiggle the iron, or your transfer will come out blurry.
3. Trace each daffodil onto tracing paper. Cut the flowers apart.
4. Transfer each daffodil onto the light yellow fabric.
5. Cut out each daffodil, leaving a 1/4" border around the edges.
6. Turn under the extra 1/4" border on the daffodils and press. Clip the curves to make the edges turn under and press more smoothly.
7. After you are finished turning under all the edges, pin each daffodil to the table runner and baste it in place with a row of loose running stitches close to the edge of the daffodil. These will be removed later on, so don't make them too tiny or permanent!
8. Using an embroidery hoop, appliqué the daffodils to the runner with all-purpose sewing thread that matches your daffodils, using the appliqué stitch (page 54).
9. Repeat Steps 3–8 with the dark yellow parts of the daffodil and the leaves. Take care to trace all of the embroidery markings (like the middle of the daffodils and the line down the middle of the leaves) onto each appliqué piece as well.
10. Embroider the runner, using the pattern at left and the photo at the beginning of the book as a guide for stitches and colors. The straight lines are outline stitches, the dots are French knots, and the loops that look like small leaves are chain stitches (see pages 52–54).
11. Connect the work on one end of the runner to the other with a long line of outline stitches that leads from one section of black embroidery to the other.

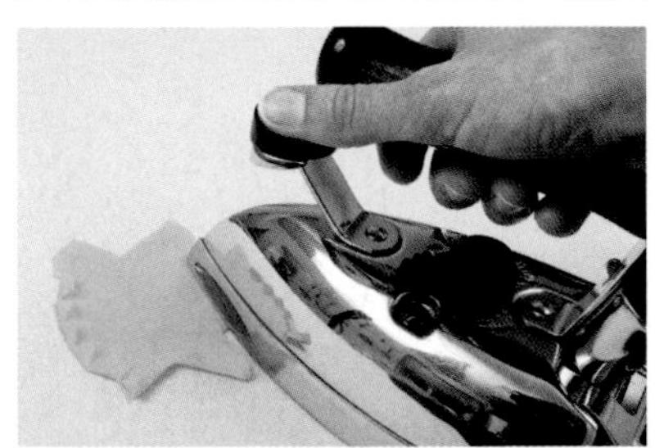

Plate Savers

Women used to crochet different-size doilies to protect their treasured sets of china, placing one between each plate when stacking them for storage or display in a china cupboard to prevent scratches and chips. Just learnin' to crochet or need a refresher? See my crochet primer—everything from positioning your hands, to basic and more complicated stitches, to attaching pieces together—complete with both photos and drawings, starting on page 118.

Supply List

No. 40 cotton crochet thread in color of your choice
Finely woven fabric for centers
Size 13 (.75 mm) steel crochet hook
1 spool all-purpose sewing thread

Gauge: Finished crochet edging is 1 1/8" wide from edge of fabric to outer edge of crochet. (You'll notice in the photo at left that the large plate has a wider crocheted edging. You can increase the number of rounds in this pattern for a wider edging, if desired. Just repeat Rnds 2–6 to desired width, then finish with Rnd 7.)

Instructions

1. To make plate savers, first cut out pieces of fabric the size and shape of the middle of your plates, saucers, bowls, and platters (refer to photo at left). Finish fabric edges with a machine straight stitch (do not hem), and then trim close to the stitches.
2. Insert crochet hook directly into fabric on the inside of the machine stitching and pull thread through. Work 2 sc in each hole that you make around right side of material, and sl st to join.

Rnd 1: Ch 6 (counts as dc plus ch 3), *sk 1 sc, dc, ch 3, repeat from * around. Sl st to join.
Rnd 2: Ch 3, sk ch-3 sp, *4 dc in next ch-3 sp (shell), sk sp, [tr in next dc, ch 2] 4 times, tr in next dc, sk ch-3 sp, repeat from * around. Join with sl st to top of first shell.
Rnd 3: *Ch 3, [sc in 3-ch sp, ch 3] 4 times, ch 3, sc in top of shell, repeat from * around. Sc in first sp made to complete the round.
Rnd 4: *Ch 5, sc in first ch-3 sp, ch 5, skip next sp, sc in next 3-ch sp, ch 5, sc in same sp, ch 5, sk sp, sc in next 3-ch sp, repeat from * around. End round by omitting last sc in 3-ch sp.
Rnd 5: *4 dc in first 5-ch sp (shell), sk sp, [tr, ch 3] 4 times, tr in same sp, sk next sp, repeat from * around. End with sl st in first shell made.
Rnd 6: *[Ch 4, sc in ch-3 sp] 4 times, ch 4, sc in top of shell, repeat from * around, ending with sc in last ch-3 sp.
Rnd 7: *Ch 5, sl st in fourth chain from hook (picot made), ch 3, sc in next sp, repeat from * around. Sl st to join. Fasten off.

If crocheting a set of Plate Savers isn't on your calendar, use vintage doilies instead.

Crocheted Head Wrap

(As seen on MaryJane on page 141.)

This pattern is a good starting place for your first head wrap because it's simple. However, any edging pattern made approximately 2" wide with two identical outer "edges" will also work. You can also find two additional head wrap patterns on my website at www.maryjanesfarm.org/StitchingRoom. But if you can't wait until you're done making your own head wrap, Wendy Harbaugh offers several different lengths and patterns in many different colors, www.vintagethreads.etsy.com, 801-722-4980.

Supplies

No. 10 cotton crochet thread
Size 4 (2 mm) steel crochet hook

Ch 35.
Row 1: Sc in eleventh ch from hook, *ch 5, skip 5 ch, sc in next ch* across row. Ch 5, turn.
Row 2: Sc in first loop, *ch 5, sc in next loop* across. Ch 5, turn.
Row 3: Repeat Row 2 until you reach the desired length. Finish off.
Border: Attach yarn in any corner loop with a slip stitch, 3 sc in loop, *sc in next sc, 3 sc in next loop* around.

Garden Trellis *Dishtowels*

Supply List

5 lint-free, superabsorbent, plain white flour-sack towels, washed (www.linens-n-things.com)

Cotton embroidery thread in colors of your choice

Tracing paper

Red wax transfer pencil

Instructions

(Refer to pages 52–54 for stitches.)

1. Trace the enlarged designs with a wax pencil onto tracing paper. Lay the tracing paper upside down on the corners of the dishtowels and iron, using the wool setting (no steam), transferring the designs onto the towels.
2. Use the outline, French knot, and chain stitches to create your designs.

Make copies of the embroidery patterns on these pages; then enlarge them 175 percent for your MaryJanesFarm dishtowel patterns.

Bias Tape *Dishtowels*

Fifties fashion ... fetching farmgirl frugality at its fanciful finest ...

It's amazing what you can do with a foot or two of rickrack or bias tape! My favorite pair of earrings are made from rickrack scraps with a rhinestone glued in the center (I even wore them when I was on my first TV talk show in Chicago). Rhinestones to riches! In that same vein, creating bias tape dishtowels is a good way to use up remnant pieces of tape and rickrack. Gather up your odds and ends and get creative designing birds, flower pots, barns, fences, and fields. Embellish them with embroidery to your heart's content. No two will ever be the same!

Wrapping Outside the Box

It took me almost forty years to "get over" boxes and wrapping paper. For a while I tried to save and recycle wrapping paper by using double-sided tape, but the pieces I saved were never the right size, and lumpy gifts still needed the right-size box. Try telling a child on Christmas morning to slow down long enough not to rip the paper! When I decided to break my wrapping paper habit once and for all, I bought dozens of sturdy paper sacks—the kind with handles—in different sizes. I embellish the sacks with "sewie" things from my stitching room: bias tape, rickrack, ribbons, buttons, etc. Instead of stuffing tissue paper into the top to hide the gift, I use torn strips of fabric. When I have a really big box to wrap, I pink the edges of some fabric to wrap it in, securing the fabric with ribbon. I especially like wired ribbon because it's so easy to mold into different shapes. The sacks flatten and store easily and can be endlessly recycled, along with the embellishments. Not only am I being less wasteful, but the sacks speed things up, leaving me plenty of time to show off my creativity by making my own cards. And the sewie things? Sometimes they find their way onto a pinkeeper, an apron ... a dishtowel or two!

Cracklejack Popcorn

A quick and easy treat for movie night, game night, or around the campfire.

1/2	cup organic popcorn kernels
1/4	cup butter
1/4	cup sugar
1	tablespoon brewed coffee

Mix butter, sugar, and brewed coffee in small saucepan. Bring to a rolling boil and cook for about 5 minutes, or until thickened. Pop kernels in an air popper or microwave. Drizzle caramel mixture over cooked popcorn. (Optional: sprinkle lightly with salt.)

Yield: 14 cups

Educational Play: Child and Nature

Our friends Ken and Jann Kolsbun believe that playing games and having a relationship with the natural world is essential to a child's development. They are devoted to supplying parents, their children, and teachers with educational and cooperative board games, outdoor play things, books, and films through their company, Child and Nature. Visit them on the Web at http://childandnature.com.

Stolen Summer Nights

If I were playing a game of Clue, I'd guess prime time to be the prime suspect that robs us of family time. My family still laughs about the time I took it upon myself to curb family TV time. I was raising my children without a TV when I started dating my neighbor and future husband, Nick Ogle. Harvest was coming up, and for economic reasons, my sweetie and I were going to harvest his crops without help—six hundred acres of wheat and peas. We planned on taking turns driving the grain truck and the combine for the four weeks it would take us to harvest his crops. We were both single parents, so it was only logical for my two youngsters (ages eight and twelve) to hang with his two youngsters (ages ten and fourteen), but in my opinion, his children watched too much TV and played too many electronic games.

One day while everyone was out and about, I used a screwdriver to take the back off his TV console and pull a few wires. Darned if that TV just wouldn't work the next time someone tried to turn it on. I took the kids to the library, gave them harvest chores, and bought a trampoline. Within a week, though, Nick's oldest son had broken his leg on the trampoline, and because of the type of break he suffered, the doctor said he'd have to lie flat on his back for at least ten days. I mumbled something about knowing how to fix TVs, and put the wires back where I'd found them. When that didn't fix it, I called in the professionals. "Well, with those wires yanked," the repairman said, "the tube itself suffered permanent damage the first time someone tried to turn it on."

With the TV permanently out of commission, his children had no choice but to follow suit, so to speak, following the lead of my children. They learned to enjoy card and board games, they puzzled together, they improvised, but more important, they bonded better. My daughter and Nick's son were eventually college roommates, our blended "blend" became more homogenized, and to this day we *all* contend it has everything to do with those four weeks they were left alone together without a TV.

> "TV. If kids are entertained by two letters, imagine the fun they'll have with twenty-six. Open your child's imagination. Open a book. Play a game."
>
> –Anonymous

My Mother's Crocheted Tablecloth

In the fifties, women took great pride in their card tables! Not only were they used for constant gaming, they were also used to seat extra dinner guests. For that reason, my mother always had several matching sets of tablecloths and napkins for adorning ours. If you're just learnin' to crochet or need a refresher, see my crochet primer on page 118.

Supply List

No. 30 cotton crochet thread in color of your choice
Size 12/1.00 mm steel crochet hook
2 yards of 60"-wide fabric for tablecloth and napkins (adjust to fit your table), washed

Assembling, Stitching, and Finishing Details

1. Start by measuring and cutting your fabric to the size of tablecloth and napkins you desire. The napkins pictured are 11" square, a good size for normal day-to-day things or snacks or cocktails. If you want something a bit more formal, you could make your napkins a little larger—be creative! For the tablecloth, measure one you already have for the table you'd like to cover, or make up a new measurement: width plus the amount hanging down doubled, by length plus the amount hanging down doubled. If

you want your tablecloth to be larger than 60" wide (the widest length you can usually purchase normal fabric in), consider cutting up an old sheet.

2. Now you're ready to start crocheting! Start with the right side of the napkin facing you. Insert your crochet hook directly into the fabric at the the top right corner inside of the machine stitching and pull your thread through.

Rnd 1: Sc into the fabric at 1/4" intervals around; sl st to first sc at beginning of rnd.

Rnd 2: Ch 3, 2 dc into first st, ch 3, 3 dc into next st, sk 3 sts, *3 dc into next st, ch 3, 3 dc into next st, sk 3 sts* (this pattern creates a little modified shell), repeat from * to * until 3 sts remain, sk last 3 sts, and sl st to first shell of rnd. Note: If you don't have exactly the correct number of stitches in your first round, don't worry. Before you round the last corner, count your remaining stitches and try to spread out the remaining shell patterns evenly. Just skip one more or one less stitch between shells. As long as they are spread out fairly evenly and not clumped together at the end, your napkin will look great!

Rnd 3: Sl st into first 3 sts of the previous rnd, ch 3, 3 dc into 3-ch sp, ch 3, sl st into first chain you just made (creates a little picot), 4 dc into 3-ch sp, *4 dc into 3-ch sp, ch 3, sl st into first chain you just made (another little picot), 4 dc into 3-ch sp,* repeat from * to * until all 3-ch spaces are filled up, sl st to beg of rnd. Fasten off.

Bean Bag Women

I couldn't believe I'd finally found another "bagger," and a better bagger at that, when my UPS driver delivered a package and a five-page letter from Donna McEvers.

Donna gifted me some bean bags along with instructions for making them. These triangle-shaped bags (she fills hers with rice and sometimes sand if there's a chance they might break open in a household with toddlers capable of choking on a bean or a kernel of rice) are embroidered with animals, flowers, birds, quotes for storytelling, and letters and numbers for spelling and counting—a kid's "hot potato." "We get the stink blowed off," Donna said about the use of bags in her family. "We invent relay games, balance them on our heads, and juggle them." If her son forgets to feed the cat, she lobs him a reminder bag, turning nagging into a parent/child memorable moment.

In my parent's living room, we had a permanent bean bag game that my father made ("early-childhood décor," my mother called it), but the bags lived everywhere around our home, becoming a lighthearted part of many of our conversations.

I took the lobbing to new heights when raising my own children. Given that our living room and kitchen weren't separated, I'd lob (gently) a broccoli floret or carrot their way while fixing meals (sometimes even a tomato or banana for honing their "pay attention, think quick, eat nutritious" skills). We got so carried away one night, we decided to actually "test" the doneness of our spaghetti on our ceiling. It did, in fact, stick, proving it was ready to eat. And as a reminder to keep our lives lighthearted, I left the noodles up there for years. My kids *loved* pointing out to their friends how "cool" their mother was to let them throw spaghetti on the ceiling!

Donna, wherever you are out there, I hope you see this! Thanks a million for "bean" such a cool mother! Together, I think we're going to create more Bam! Bean-oh's.

TUCO
Picture Puzzle

Stitching
Around the House

Yo!

Pieces of scrap fabric cut into circles and gathered in the center are referred to as yo-yos. Yo-yo quilts are a fabulous way to use up all those scraps of fabric you have tucked away. (The farmgirls on our chatroom call them UFOs: unfinished fabric objects!) Since they are made without batting and aren't actually quilted or even backed, they're more like coverlets than quilts. They can be made to any size or shape. Fabric circles are very portable, so throw a few in your handbag that can be worked into yo-yos the next time you're waiting for an appointment, riding the bus, or just sitting on the porch enjoying a summer evening.

1. Decide how large you want your yo-yos to be. The raw fabric circle is nearly twice the size of the finished yo-yo. Use any flat, circular object as a template. A plastic container lid, plate, CD, cup, can, etc., all work. (A 4 1/2" CD makes an ideal template for roughly a 2" yo-yo.) Experiment until you get the size you want for your project.
2. Cut out the circle. Fold the edge under 1/4" and press, or just fold the edge over as you stitch. With the wrong side of the fabric facing up and starting from the back, make a short running stitch all the way around the circle. For best results, keep your stitches close to the folded edge of the fabric. When you have stitched all the way around the circle, carefully start pulling the thread so the circle gathers toward the center. Keep pulling until you have a pouch with gathered edges and a little opening in the middle. Flatten the pouch and center the hole, adjusting the gathers if they are too tight or too loose. Knot the thread to hold the yo-yo securely.
3. When you have made a stack of yo-yos, you can stitch them together (just tack on four sides) to make a quilt of any size. Or have fun using them to embellish clothing, purses, pillowcases, ponytail elastics, dishtowels, curtains, or anything else (see following pages)!

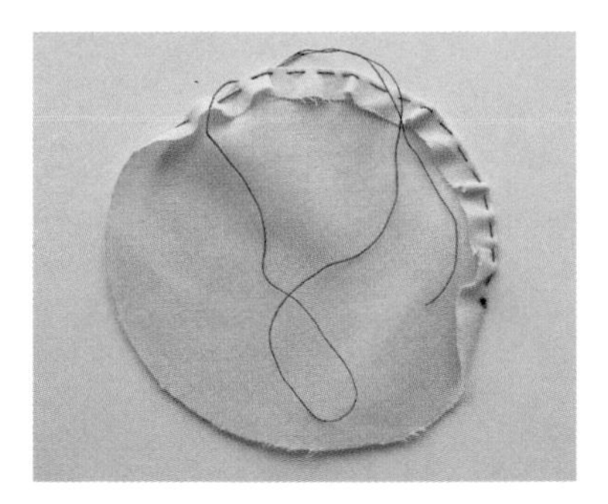

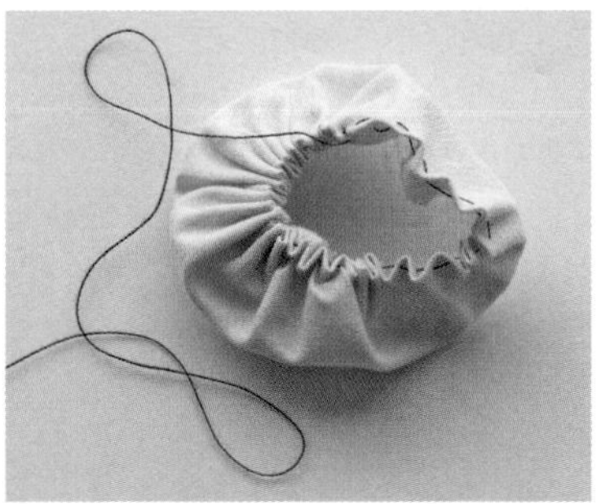

Note: Longer stitches allow the fabric to gather together more closely, creating a smaller center; shorter stitches create a larger, more open center.

The yo-yo clown pictured above (complete with bells for hands and feet) has been a cherished friend to our dear Cindylou since she was six years old, a gift from her great aunt Molly (a very dignified woman who was never seen in public without a veiled hat and dress gloves). Cindylou's job here at the farm is to help coordinate all the farmgirl chapters sprouting up around the world. As of last count, there were nearly four hundred. For more information about how to join or start a farmgirl chapter, go to our website, www.maryjanesfarm.org.

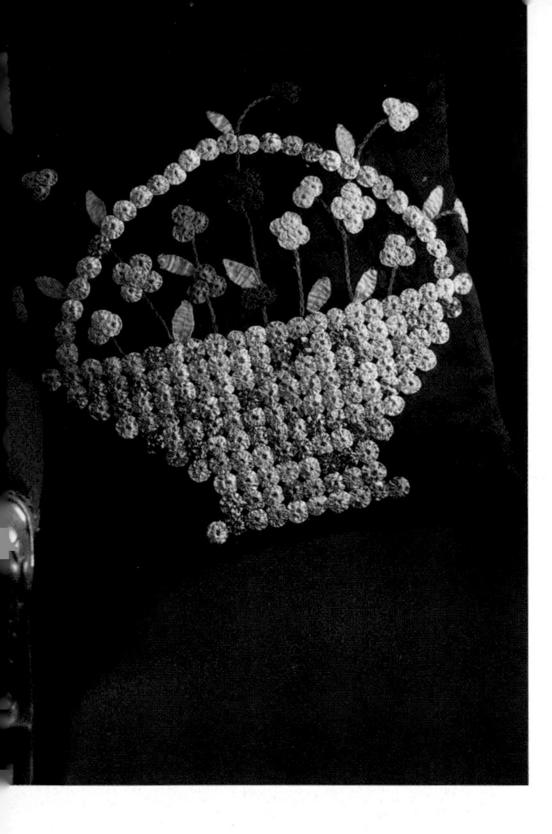

Yo-Yo Pillow

Supply List

2 16"-square pieces of fabric for the body of the pillow
220 yo-yos made from 1 1/2" circles of fabric (about 50 from a solid fabric and the rest from a print; see yo-yo directions on page 47)
1 6"-square scrap of green fabric for leaves
Green embroidery floss
All-purpose sewing thread
Stuffing for pillow or 15"-square pillow form

Instructions

1. Using the photo at top left and on page 44 as a guide, start by sewing twenty-two of your yo-yos together in a straight line by tacking them together side by side. This is the very top row of the basket. Sew the next row of yo-yos together (twenty this time; each row will have one less yo-yo on each side), and then tack them to the first row. Following the photograph, repeat until the basket is finished.
2. Sew your basket to one of the squares of fabric for the body of the pillow by tacking each yo-yo in the middle and then around the edges of the whole basket. Center it in the middle from side to side and place the bottom of the basket about 2 1/2" away from the bottom edge of your fabric.
3. Thread a needle with four strands of green embroidery floss. Create the flower stems coming out of the basket with a chain stitch (see page 53). Use our photo as a guide or be creative on your own! Just remember that there is a 5/8" seam allowance, so don't get too close to the edge of the fabric.
4. Sew yo-yos in groups of two or more to the ends of the chain-stitch stems you made. Also, sew a few groups right over the stems.
5. Make a handful of leaves (ten or so) from your green fabric. Just cut out an oblong shape that is pointed on both ends and about 2" long and 1" wide. Turn the edges of your leaves under 1/4" and press. Position the leaves so they look as if they are growing off the flowers' stems. Sew them to the pillow using all-purpose sewing thread and a tiny running stitch, or if you are feeling a bit more decorative, stitch close to the edge of the leaf with two strands of embroidery floss, using a running stitch.
6. Lastly, sew twenty-seven or so yo-yos into a straight line. This will be the handle of your basket, so position it as shown and sew in place.
7. With the right sides of your two squares of pillow fabric together, sew along three sides with a 5/8" seam allowance. Turn right side out. Stuff your pillow or place your pillow form inside, and stitch the last side closed by hand, turning the raw edges to the inside.

With just two yo-yos, you can add a bit of crochet and a button, and you've got a lapel pin like the one at left. I don't buy fancy hooks for my adornments; I just sew a safety pin on the back!

For gifts, my mother made hundreds of padded hangers covered in yo-yos.

A yo-yo married to a button creates a lovely certerpiece for a pinkeeper.

Here's a unique card idea using a yo-yo!

If life is a dance, every sure-footed farmgirl needs a yo-yo embellished skirt to twirl in!

When Things Get Crazy ... Make a Pillow!

"Sometimes you need chaos in your soul to give birth to a dancing star."

– Friedrich Wilhelm Nietzsche

Supply List

Fabric scraps
Embroidery floss
Thread
Embroidery needles
Embroidery hoop (optional)
Muslin for lining
Backing fabric
Batting or pillow form

Assembling, Stitching, and Finishing Details

1. Although this type of quilting doesn't need batting, you will need a muslin lining and a backing to make a pillow (velvet is an elegant backing). Decide what size you'd like your pillow to be and cut the muslin and the backing to this size. Don't forget to add enough of a seam allowance on all four sides to sew the front piece onto the back of the pillow. Collect scraps of fabric. Satin and velvet are beautiful in crazy quilts and can be mixed with pieces of corduroy, flannel, ribbon, lace, old ties, shirts, wool skirts, etc., for your pillow.
2. Lay out the muslin on a flat surface and begin covering it with your scraps, like a puzzle. Pieces can be cut into triangles, squares, rectangles, or any other shapes to create a pillow the desired size. Overlap the pieces 1/2" and turn under the raw edges on the top pieces. You may want to start with one scrap in the middle and then build onto it piece by piece, basting as you go, until the muslin is covered. Trim away seam allowances, extra fabric, and any scraps that hang over the edges of the muslin to create straight edges.
3. Now be creative! Join the pieces together using embroidery stitches (I've given you instructions for my favorites on the following pages). You may want to use one stitch for the whole pillow, or many different types of stitches for a "crazier" look. Choose different colors of embroidery thread that complement the different fabrics. The embroidery stitches are functional as well as decorative, because they hold all of the pieces together. Every seam should be covered with some type of embroidery stitch. You can also select several patches to embroider with flowers or other designs and details.
4. Turn under all four sides of the pillow front 1/4" and press. Turn under all four sides of the pillow backing 1/4" and press. Pin together the front piece and the back piece with wrong sides together. Baste three sides. Sew three sides of the front onto the back using an embroidery stitch (blanket or herringbone work well). Fill the pillowcase with batting or a pillow, then baste and sew up the remaining side with an embroidery stitch.

Crazy quilts make use of beautiful leftover scraps of fabric and act as a showcase for unusual and unique embroidery stitches.

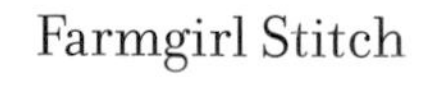

Farmgirl Stitch

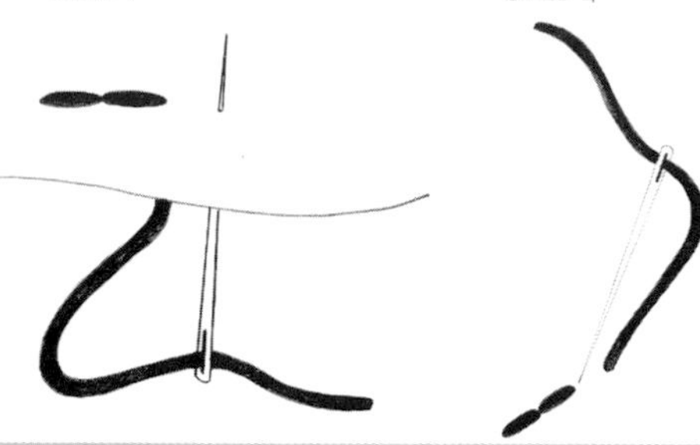

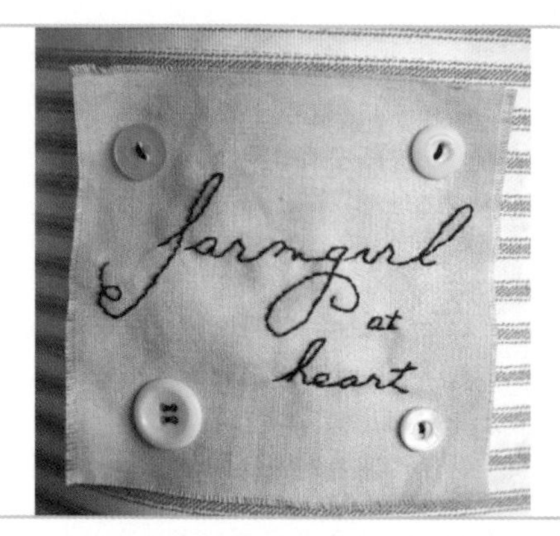

Straight Stitch

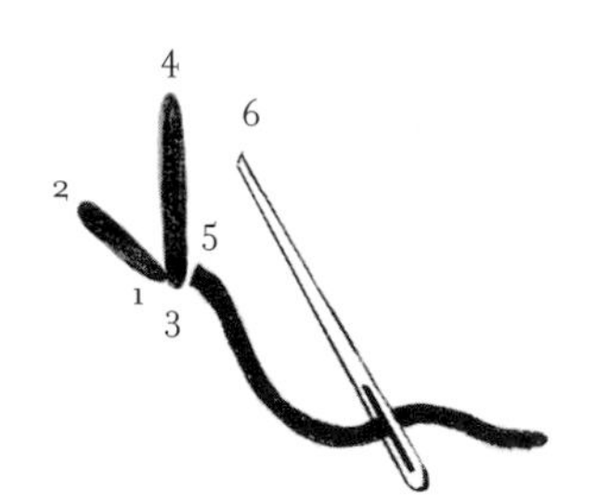

Blanket Stitch

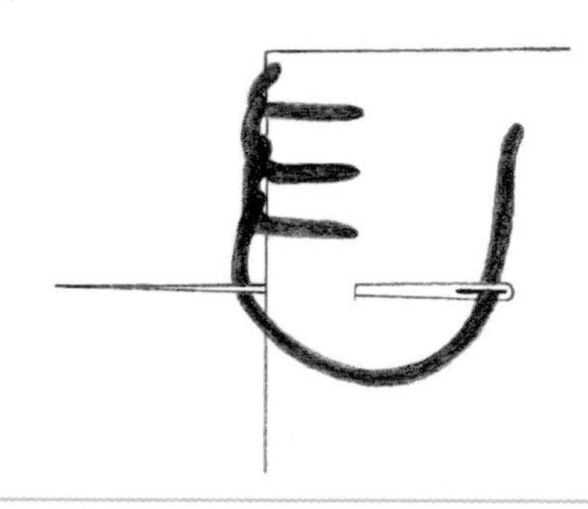

French Knot

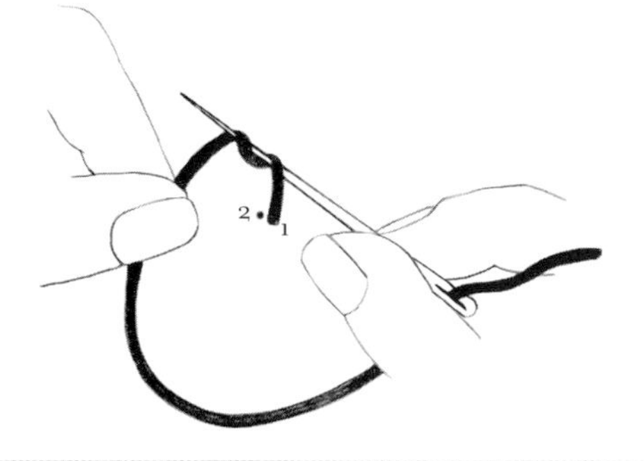

Come up at 1. Pull thread through. With finger and thumb on your hand that is not holding the needle, wrap the thread around the needle two or three times. Keeping the thread taut, rotate the needle down toward the fabric and insert it right next to 1 at 2. Pull through, keeping the knot on the right side of fabric.

Chain Stitch

STEP 1

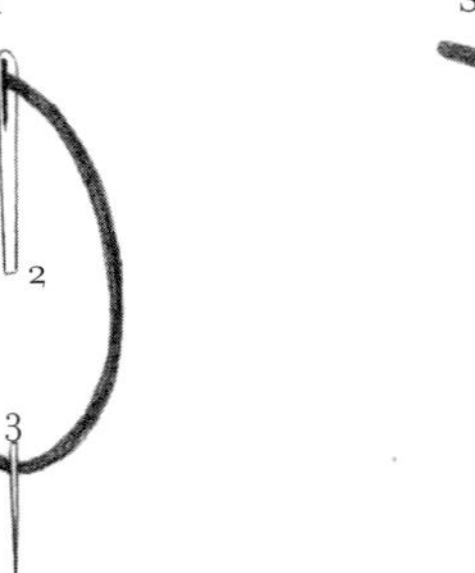

STEP 2

STEP 3

Herringbone Stitch

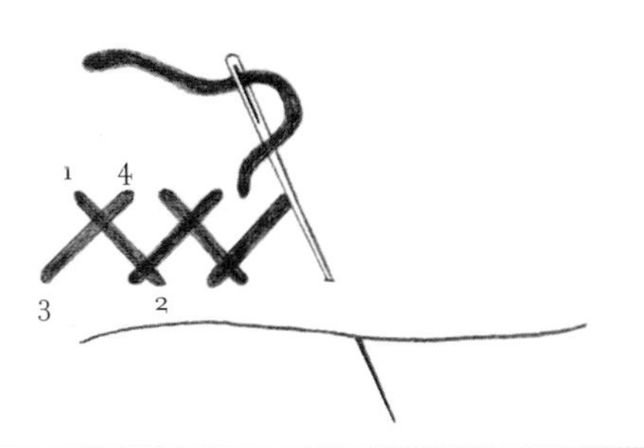

Crazy embroidery stitches can also be used to gussy up jean pockets or as a playful embellishment along the hem of a skirt.

Lazy Daisy Stitch

STEP 1

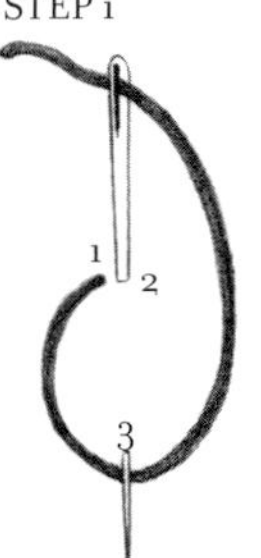

STEP 2

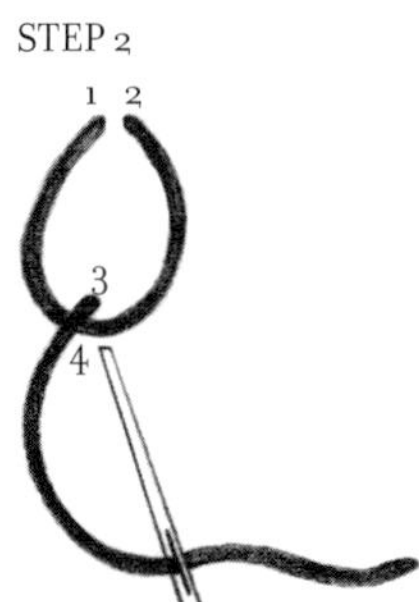

STEP 3

Feather Stitch

STEP 1

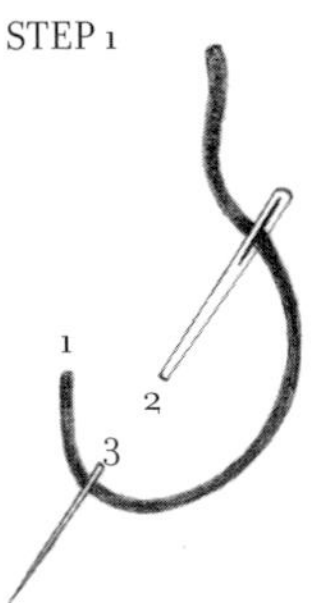

STEP 2

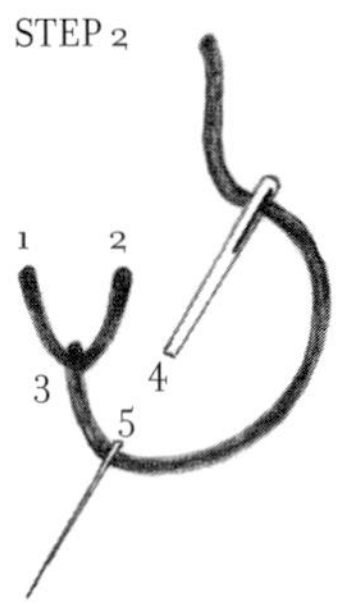

STEP 3

Outline Stitch

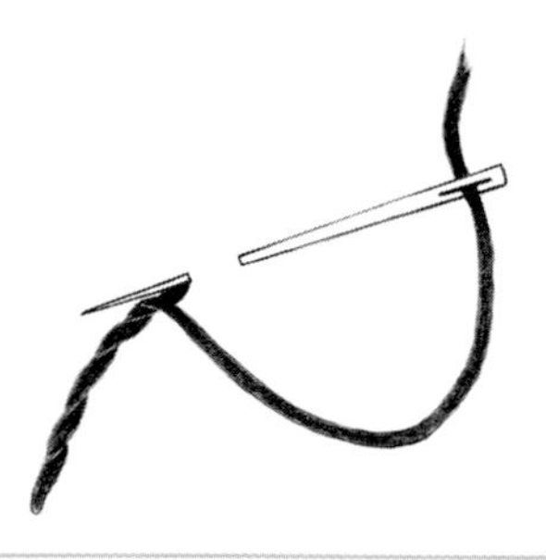

Filler Stitch

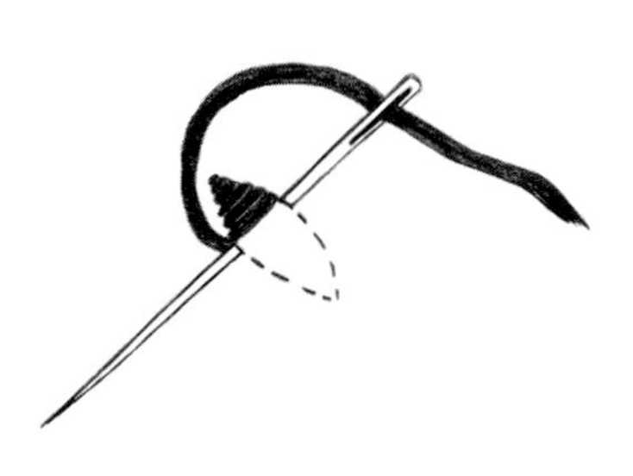

Buttonhole Stitch

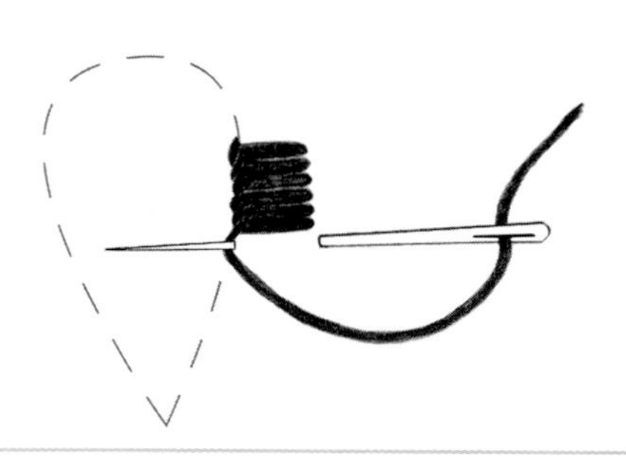

After you've outlined your design with buttonhole stitches, cut the middle out with a very sharp pair of small scissors.

Appliqué Stitch

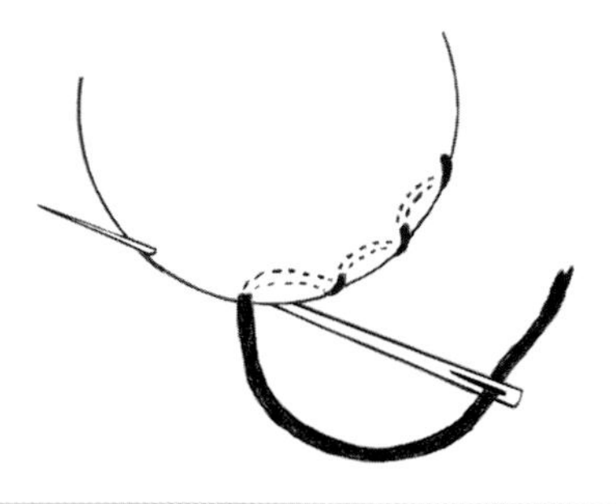

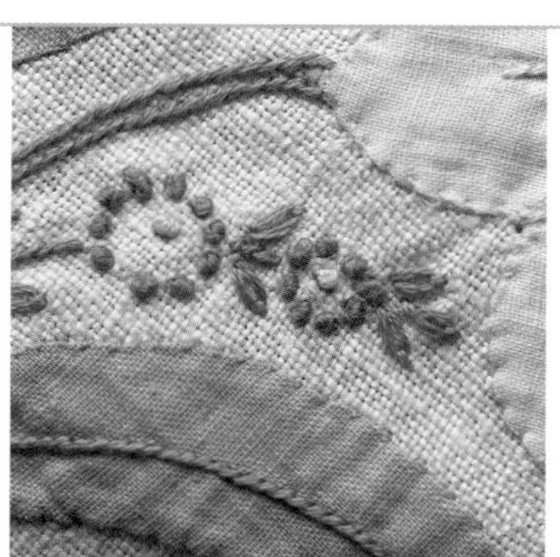

Farmgirl Fabulous

Julia Hayes is pure farmgirl inspiration—especially when she greets you on her tractor (a surprise fortieth birthday gift from her husband) with painted lips and wearing the dress and shawl she stitched for herself when her doctor husband asked her to abandon her usual overalls and attend a fancy medical convention with him. Joyous beyond measure and uplifting (before she became a mother, she traveled to Europe as the eyes and ears of a blind and hearing-impaired woman), Julia is one lit-up farmgirl, full of enthusiasm for life. Julia sews clothes that she peddles at local fairs, each of which comes with a hand-stitched tag that reads "being simple to simply be." Even the size tags are hand embroidered. Julia also made the hand-stitched card on page 39 using dried pumpkin seeds. (What a great idea!) We *love* the image of Julia plowing snow or moving compost in her overalls as guests arrive, but always ready to entertain with an apron beneath her "farm-alls." She and her mother painted the walls in her son's bedroom as a farm scene (another good idea!). The closet doors are "barn" doors, complete with life-size chickens lined up and ready for breakfast.

One of my favorite stitchery authors is Kristen Nicholas. The creative director of a yarn company for almost twenty years, she knows more about textiles than we farmgirls ever will. Kristen says, "Stitching is a life in its own. It will hold you together when you're falling apart. I can't live without stitching. It has become the one constant in my life that I always carry with me, to all reaches of the globe."

Rags to Rugs & Bags

Whittling Away

For most people, the word whittling brings to mind a general store with old men out front, their conversation punctuated by flying wood chips. My image is that of my grandma Butters (Artie) getting out her pocketknife and whittling animals, clothespin dolls, toy boats, walking sticks, buttons, Christmas ornaments, signs, spoons—anything her gentle hands and imaginative mind could dream up. When I was too young to handle a sharp knife (the only rule to whittling), she got me started by handing me a table knife, some wax candles, and a bar of soap. Artie was a "reel" woman, meaning she fished. The two of us would sit for hours by the side of a lake, our bobbers cast, whittling away. Zucchini boats complete with wooden masts and a Barbie bunk became my specialty. I took to sending my Barbie doll sailing down irrigation ditches near my home—the more culverts, the better.

My father, also a whittler, was fond of sharp knives. "A sharp knife is safer than a dull knife. Since it's harder to cut with a dull knife, you apply more pressure. The more pressure you apply, the more likely you are to cut yourself," my dad taught.

I whittle toward myself, carving with a small Swiss Army pocket knife I've had for thirty-five years and using my thumb as a stop for the blade. This method is very natural. It allows you to control how deep you go. If you're nervous about cutting yourself, wear a leather thimble on your thumb.

To make a crochet hook for a rag rug, choose a close-grained scrap of wood (I used the rung from an old chair back). Pieces of driftwood will also work. You want to end up with a dowel that is roughly 1/2" in diameter and 6" to 7" long. The hook at the end needs to be 3/8" to 1/2" wide with about a 1/8" gap. It's as simple as that. But hey, if you aren't inclined to whittle (I do encourage you to at least try), you can buy a hook. A size L/11 (8mm) on up to a size P/16 (11.5 mm) crochet hook will work just fine.

> "When our eyes see our hands doing the work of our hearts, the circle of creation is completed inside us, the doors of our souls fly open, and love steps forth to heal everything in sight."
>
> — Anne Jones

Crocheted Rag Rug

For fabric, choose lightweight cotton (old sheets are ideal). I prefer to rip my fabric into 1 1/2" strips rather than cut it with scissors. The messy strings don't bother me. I use scissors to make a starter cut, then rip. Better yet, if you have a rotary cutter and table mat, you can cut through several layers of fabric at once. To join the pieces of fabric as I create balls of strips, I cut a 1/2" lengthwise opening in the end of each strip (like a buttonhole) and pull the next strip through that opening—like putting two rubber bands together. This method of joining won't work once you're actually making your rug and need to switch to a new ball. I merely tie them together using a square knot, but you can hand stitch them together if you want.

Instructions

Ch 10.

Work a sc into each st. Work 3 more sc into the last ch, then work a sc into the other side of each ch to make an oval shape. Keep going in a big spiral until your rug is as large as you want it. If your rug starts to curl, simply work a few additional sc along the curves. It's very forgiving and encourages individuality!

Note: It is customary when crocheting to pick up the two top threads of every stitch. When only the front stitch is picked up, a different effect is produced. My rag rug is made with only the front stitch picked up from start to finish.

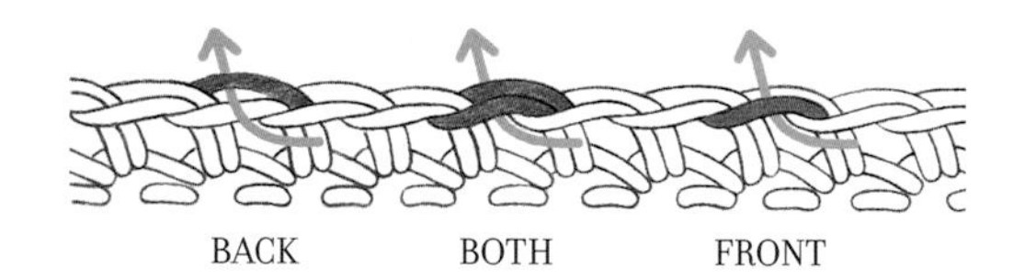

Eco-tip:

You can also use plastic grocery bags to create a shoulder bag. Using the pattern at right and an M hook, simply cut the handles and the bottom seam from dozens of bags. Fold each bag into a strip. Cut into 2" pieces. Connect the resulting "rings," one ring inserted into the end of the other—reminiscent of joining rubber bands when you were a kid. Gently pull ring after ring together, forming "knots" in a continuous strand of plastic. Repeat. Roll your strips into balls of "yarn."

Just learnin' to crochet or need a refresher? See my crochet primer—with everything from positioning your hands, to basic and more complicated stitches, to attaching pieces together—complete with both photos and drawings, starting on page 118.

Crocheted Rag Bag

Supply List

10 yards 45"-wide fabric, washed (This bag used 5 yards of print and 5 yards of solid material.)

Size M/13 (9 mm) crochet hook

Small amount of 4-ply yarn

Instructions

Body of Bag

Row 1: With solid color, ch 31 (for smaller bag, simply decrease number of chain stitches), hdc in third chain from hook, ch 2, turn.

Row 2: Hdc in each hdc across, ch 2, turn.

Row 3: Working in print fabric, repeat Row 2 until piece reaches 9 1/2". Work in solid color and crochet 3 more rows. Fasten off. Repeat for second side of bag.

Handle, Side, and Bottom of Bag

Row 1: Ch 4, turn. Sc in second ch from hook and next 2 ch, ch 1, turn.

Row 2: Sc in 3 sc across, ch 1, turn.

Rows 3–: Repeat Row 2 until piece is approximately 68" long.

Finishing

Using 4-ply yarn, start at center bottom of bag, matching rows, and sc in each sc to corner. Work 3 sc in corner, and matching rows, sc up side of bag. Fasten off at top of bag. Repeat for other half of bottom of bag and side. Sew bottom center of bag together. Tie in all ends.

Flower Pillow

Just learnin' to crochet or need a refresher? See my crochet primer—everything from positioning your hands, to basic and more complicated stitches, to attaching pieces together—complete with both photos and drawings, starting on page 118.

Supply List

1 skein Red Heart Soft Baby in Powder Yellow (A)
1 skein Bernat Softee Baby in 02003 Lemon (B)
1 skein Encore 4-ply worsted in 146 Beige (C)
1 skein Red Heart Soft Baby in Lime (D)
Size G/6 (4.25 mm) crochet hook
Tapestry needle
18"-x-18" square pillow covered in muslin or sheeting

Gauge: Granny square = 4" square

Instructions

Granny square:

1. Ch 4 using A, join chain with a sl st to form a ring.

Rnd 1: (right side) Ch 3 (counts as a dc), work 2 dc into ring, ch 2, *work 3 dc into ring, ch 2, repeat from * 2 more times. Join round with a sl st in third chain of ch-3. Fasten off. From wrong side, join next color (B) with a sl st in any ch-2 sp.

Rnd 2: Ch 3, work 2 dc in same ch-2 sp, ch 1, *work [3 dc, ch 2, 3 dc] in next ch-2 sp, ch 1, repeat from * 2 more times, end with 3 dc in beginning ch-2 sp, ch 2, join round with a sl st in third chain of ch-3. Fasten off. From right side, join next color (C) with a sl st in any ch-2 sp.

Rnd 3: Ch 3, work 2 dc in same ch-2 sp, ch 1, *work 3 dc in next ch-1 sp, ch 1, work [3 dc, ch 2, 3 dc] in next ch-2 sp, ch 1, repeat from * 2 more times, end with 3 dc in next ch-1 sp, ch 1, 3 dc in beginning ch-2 sp, ch 2. Join round with a sl st in third chain of ch-3. Fasten off. From wrong side, join next color (B) with a sl st in any ch-2 sp.

Rnd 4: Ch 3, work 2 dc in same ch-2 sp, ch 1, *work [3 dc in next ch-1 sp, ch 1] twice, work [3 dc, ch 2, 3 dc] in next ch-2 sp, ch 1, repeat from * 2 more times, end with [3 dc in next ch-1 sp, ch 1] twice, 3 dc in beginning ch-2 sp, ch 2. Join round with a sl st in third chain of ch-3. Fasten off.

2. Crochet another granny square for the back side of pillow.

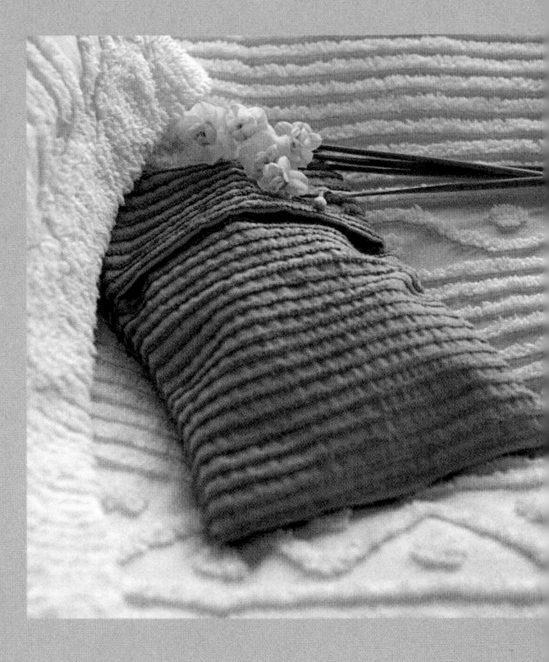

Hot Water Bottle Cover

A nuturing accent for a guest room.

Supply List

3/8 yard 45"-wide cotton chenille fabric, washed
1 spool all-purpose sewing thread

Cutting

Cut one 34"-x-10" rectangle

Assembling, Stitching, and Finishing Details

1. Hem top and bottom (short) edges with a 1/2" seam.
2. With right sides together, fold top down 5 1/2" and bottom up 12 1/2". Stitch both sides through all three layers. Turn right side out.
3. Flip top open and slide hot water bottle in. Flip top closed as you would a pillow sham, with the hot water bottle inserted like a pillow.

Baby Slings

Sling-style infant carriers are used throughout the world for good reason—soothed by movement and close contact, babies stay happier. But when it comes to slings, simple is better. Modern versions of this age-old device are unnecessarily complicated. Rebekka Boysen-Taylor, who is a regular u-pick visitor to my farm, taught herself how to sew when she was pregnant with her daughter and living in L.A. "I had an uncontrollable urge for things made by hand, with love." Moving back home to the Northwest, she made the decision to be a stay-at-home mom. That's when she started sewing baby goods in earnest, quickly picking up several store accounts. When you place an order for one of her slings, it ships with a little something extra—Rebekka's pattern—so you can sew one for your next baby shower! "I like to help women simplify and change their buying habits, one purchase at a time." www.bebebella.com, 208-882-1353.

Leaves:

1. Ch 12 using D, sc in second ch from hook, and in each of next 2 st, 2 hdc, 3 dc, 1 hdc, sc in next ch, 3 sc in last ch. Working down the other side of the original ch-12, sc in next ch, 1 hdc in next ch, 3 dc, 2 hdc, sc, sl st to next st. Fasten off, leaving a tail of about 6".
2. Repeat 7 more times.

Attaching leaves to the granny squares:

*Put leaf at corner of granny square, right sides together, attach leaf with 2 sc, ch 2; attach another leaf in the same manner on the other side of the corner, ch 20, repeat from * 3 more times. Join with a sl st at base of first leaf.

Large-weave trellis:

To do the trellis, you will work from the underside of the pillow.

Rnd 1: *Ch 15 using D, sc in next ch-20 sp, ch 15, sc in ch-2 sp, repeat from * around.

Rnd 2: *Ch 20, sc in next ch-15 sp, repeat from * around.

Rnd 3: *Ch 25, sc in next ch-20 sp, repeat from * around.

Rnd 4: Ch 17, sc in first ch-25 sp, *ch 20, sc in ch-25 sp, ch 35, sc in next ch-25 sp, repeat from * 3 more times, ch 20, sc in next ch-25 sp, ch 28, join with a sl st in ch-9 of ch-17.

Rnd 5: Ch 9 (counts as tr and ch 4), tr in first open sp, [ch 4, tr] 2 more times in same sp, *[ch 4, tr] 7 times in next sp (this is the side of the pillow), [ch 4, tr] 11 times in next sp (this is the corner of the pillow), repeat from * around 3 more times, [ch 4, tr] 7 times each in next 2 sp. Ch 4, join with a sl st in ch-5 of first ch-9.

Rnd 6 & 7: Ch 4 (counts as dc), 2 tr in first ch-4 sp, dc in same sp (shell made), ch 1, *[dc, 2 tr, dc, ch 1] in each ch-4 sp, in sixth ch-4 sp of corner do two shells. Join with a sl st in fourth ch of first st.
Fasten off.

Pillow back:

Rnd 1: Starting at far right shell of granny square, *ch 20 with D, sc in far left shell of same side of granny square, ch 2, sc in far right shell of neighboring side just worked, repeat from * 3 times, ending with a sl st in first ch made.

Rnd 2: *Ch 15, sc in next ch-20 sp, ch 15, sc in ch-2 sp, repeat from * around.

Rnd 3: *Ch 20, sc in next ch-15 sp, repeat from * around.

Rnd 4: *Ch 25, sc in next ch-20 sp, repeat from * around.

Rnd 5: Ch 17, sc in first ch-25 sp, *ch 20, sc in ch-25 sp, ch 35, sc in next ch-25 sp, repeat from * 3 more times, ch 20, sc in next ch-25 sp, ch 28, join with a sl st in ch-9 of ch-17.

Rnd 6: Ch 9 (counts as tr and ch 4), tr in first open sp, [ch 4, tr] 2 more times in same sp, *[ch 4, tr] 7 times in next sp (this is the side of the pillow), [ch 4, tr] 11 times in next sp (this is the corner of the pillow), repeat from * around 3 more times, [ch 4, tr] 7 times each in next 2 sp, ch 4, join with a sl st in ch-5 of first ch-9.

Rnd 7 & 8: Ch 4 (counts as dc), 2 tr in first ch-4 sp, dc in same sp (shell made), ch 1, *[dc, 2 tr, dc, ch 1] in each ch-4 sp, in sixth ch-4 sp of corner do two shells. Join with a sl st in fourth ch of first st. Fasten off.

Bebe Bella

...essentials by Mama for a Mama...

Mama's Nursing Bracelet

New mamahood is a beautiful, crazy time. Every now and then mama needs a little extra help to keep things balanced. This bracelet can be moved from one wrist to the other to help you remember which side baby nursed on last, especially helpful after that 3 am feeding. While it seems like a little thing it will help to prevent uncomfortable engorgement on one side. As baby gets older Mama will enjoy her nursing bracelet as a reminder of this amazing time.

Thanks for supporting a local Mama!

Rebekka and Bella

Email us at amamaswork@yahoo.com

Flower for pillow front:

1. Flower petals: Ch 12 using B, sc in second ch from hook, and in each st to last st, hdc, 2 dc, 2 tr, dc, 2 hdc, 3 sc in last ch. Working down the other side of the original ch-12, hdc in next ch, dc, 2 tr, 2 dc, hdc, 3 sc, sl st to next st. Fasten off, leaving a tail of about 6". Repeat 4 more times.

2. Flower cup: Using A, ch 5, sl st to join into ring, ch 1.

Rnd 1: 6 sc into ring, sl st to join.

Rnds 2–5: *Ch 1, 2 sc in first st, sc in rest of sts around, sl st to join. Repeat from * around for each round.

Rnds 6–8: Ch 1, sc in each st around, sl st to join.

Rnd 9: Ch 3, 4 dc in each st around. Fasten off.

3. Attach petals to cup with B, using 2 sc in each petal at base of cup. Attach flower using B to the center of the front granny square with small stitches on the underside of granny square, making sure to catch the flower in the stitch. Secure petals to the granny square with the same yarn.

Clothes Closet *Stitching*

Farmgirl *Rag Yarn Scarf*

Just learnin' to crochet or need a refresher? See my crochet primer—everything from positioning your hands, to basic and more complicated stitches, to attaching pieces together—complete with both photos and drawings, starting on page 118.

Supply List

3 skeins Schulana Zigane (bulky specialty) yarn, Tan, or similar style yarn of your choice

Size J/10 (6 mm) crochet hook

Blunt-tip needle for weaving in ends

Instructions

Ch 28.

Row 1: Work 1 dc into fourth ch from hook, work 1 dc into each ch. Turn.

Row 2: Ch 3 (counts as 1 dc), work 2 dc into first st (an increase), dc into each st until you get to last 2 sts, work 1 dc into last 2 sts (a decrease). Turn.

Row 3: Ch 3 (counts as 1 dc), work 1 dc into first 2 sts (a decrease), work 1 dc into each st until you get to the last st, work 2 dc into last st (an increase). Turn.

Rows 4–100 (or until yarn runs out): Repeat rows 2 and 3 alternately. Fasten off.

Ragamuffin Diapers

I met Kendra Parnell while visiting the Apple Family Farm in Indiana during my book tour. The mother of three children, Kendra started making cloth diapers ten years ago when someone gave her a set of flowery flannel sheets that were the wrong size for her bed. On a tight budget, she decided to repurpose them into diapers, which eventually turned into a business for her. Still using recycled fibers whenever she can find them (she refers to them as "gently used"), Kendra modeled her Ragamuffin Hand-Sewn Diapers after a disposable diaper. The easy-to-use, one-size, three-layer flannel diapers (with ten extra layers in the wet zone for absorbency) fit newborns to toddlers. For smaller babies, you simply fold the diaper front down. She also makes diaper double inserts, cloth-diaper wipes, and Velcro-wrap diaper covers.

Cloth diapering is a lost art, but switching to cloth saves money and, as Kendra points out, "If I use disposable diapers, my children and grandchildren will get stuck cleaning up a diaper mess someday. Cloth diapering teaches our children that it's easy to be better stewards of our environment." To convert today, you can reach Kendra at ragamuffindiapers@hotmail.com or at 317-924-4643. And for loads of farm romance and inspiration, visit Debbie Apple at www.applefamilyfarm.com.

Wrapping It All … In a Knitted Shawl

I met Eve Mills while on a book tour. Wrapped in the most beautiful shawl, she told me how her desire for a neck wrap to guard against Montana winters eventually morphed into a far-flung business using hand-dyed mohair that is grown and produced in Idaho by another woman entrepreneur.

To this day, she still uses only one stitch, the very basic "knit" stitch, to make her shawls, neck wraps and scarves! With boutique accounts in places like New York's Soho, she sells her creations worldwide as well as by mail order. Never before a craftsperson, she knits them in her kitchen, sending them out into the world without a label. "I always end up taking labels off when I buy something. I think they interfere with the beauty of an object."

Since Eve is determined to keep her life simple, the only way to contact her is by phone, 406-327-9802.

Multipurpose Crocheted Shawl

A versatile accessory that can be worn as a hip shawl or a head or neck scarf. If you're just learnin' to crochet or need a refresher, see my crochet primer on page 118.

Supply List

1 skein Patons Brilliant (bulky specialty) yarn, Burgundy, or similar style yarn of your choice
Size Q/19 (15 mm) crochet hook
Blunt-tip needle for working in ends
Pattern is for size small. Make your base chain 10 stitches longer for each size you would like to increase.
Gauge: 4" x 4" = 6 stitches and 5 rows worked in single crochet with front/back loop dropped

Instructions

Ch 51.
Row 1: Sk first ch and sc into each ch after. Turn.
Row 2: Ch 1, sc2tog. *Sc in next st by picking up back loop only, sc in next st by picking up front loop only.* Repeat from * to * until only 2 sts remain, sc2tog. Turn.
Remaining Rows (number differs according to size): Work the same as Row 2 until only 4 sts remain. Turn.
Second-to-last Row: Ch 1, sc2tog twice (2 sts remain). Turn.
Last Row: Ch 1, sc2tog again (1 st remains). Fasten off.

Made-to-order knitted shawls by Eve Mills, Missoula, Montana.

Farmgirl *Hex*

The hexagon, a shape that speaks the zen of the busy beehive or the wired manors of chickens (the oldest domesticated animal on earth), symbolizes the unity and structure of the farmgirl life—a framework for the proper order of things, a pattern for life. In unwritten feminine language, it is a standard for farmgirls, or for that matter, the ordinary honeybee or the hen, rank and file workers that move the work along. It says that all things are to be done decently and in order, and that small things add up.

Like some kind of primal code stamped onto my feminine DNA, the hexagon has always seemed to me to be a symbol of female order and harmony. I really didn't know why until recently. It wasn't something I learned in school or church. It didn't come from a book ... that I knew of. (The six-sided symbol from the book *The Da Vinci Code* hadn't been "discovered" yet, at least not in a best-selling book.)

After my father's death in 2003 and my mother's unexpected death in 2006, I spent four weeks alone, in their home, remembering. I sat for tea where my mother had sat. I drank from her favorite cup. I slept in her bed. I crocheted. Uneasy at first, I eventually fell asleep, lulled by the whistle of distant trains—the same, mournful, lonesome-dove sound she must have heard, alone, after Daddy died.

I played her music—Doris Day, Nat King Cole, The Platters, Rosemary Clooney, Tommy Dorsey, Patsy Cline, The Ink Spots. I sorted through her holiday decorations (all of them handmade), her sewing room. I read her journals—sixty years' worth. When I couldn't cry anymore, I sorted safety pins and paper clips, spools of thread, tangled baskets of embroidery floss. After a week or so, I started napping several times a day, like a baby again. I like to think I was hexed, in a good way—that a magical spell, an unexpected solace, had been cast my way. I settled in. I felt undisturbed and comforted, a warmth reminiscent of getting tucked in at night, right up to your chin under a familiar quilt, with a kiss to the forehead. One day I even imagined living out the rest of my life there, in my childhood home—a more simple, anonymous life, unlike my busy farm, magazine, and book life.

First it was the hexagon quilt my mother created when she was fifteen that made me sit up and take notice. Then it was a Christmas ornament here and there. Crocheted snowflakes. A hexagonal Easter basket. Several six-sided tablecloths. Hankies. Then I found hexagon place mats and hexagon pockets on aprons. I even found a six-sided open box my mother had made from old seed packets—seven hexagons three inches across (six for the sides, one for the bottom), whip-stitched together using embroidery floss.

On a hunt then for hexagons, I began to realize that my parents had left their offspring one last treasure hunt. They were famous among the children in our neighborhood for their treasure hunts leading to a pot of "gold"—"pennies from heaven." My father hid pennies in our sandbox, under rocks in creeks, under cucumbers we'd been asked to harvest, and—magician-style—pennies "behind" our ears.

First I found hundred-dollar bills tucked into a sewing pattern for a baby's burping bib, one for each of their children. Then I found a stack of twenty-dollar bills in an envelope with our names on it between some Halloween place mats in the hallway closet. A heavy sack of fabric scraps in Momma's sewing room held more than a hundred Susan B. Anthony coins. There were folders containing rare turn-of-

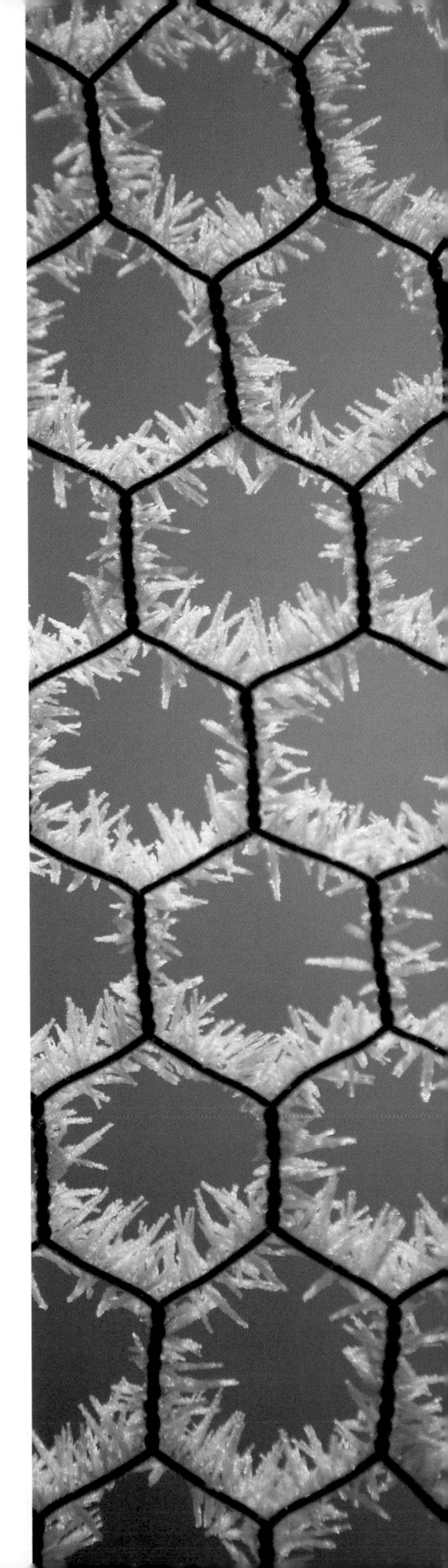

Did you know that snowflake crystals are always hexagonal and that no two are ever alike? How do we know such unity exists? In 1880, a self-educated, fifteen-year-old farmboy from Vermont started looking at snowflakes under an old teaching microscope. For three years he produced some four hundred snowflake drawings, wishing to share the true beauty of what he saw with others. Given all the chores required to run a farm back then, locals began to scoff at him. But his mother was able to persuade his father to buy him the hundred-dollar camera he dreamed of. Working in an unheated woodshed, he adapted the microscope to fit his bellows camera, held his breath so as not to melt the crystals, and for many years tried in vain to capture a snowflake on film. Finally, in 1885, Wilson Bentley captured the world's first photograph of a single snowflake. He went on to capture more than five thousand different snowflakes on film. Despite his growing recognition among meteorologists, who started calling him the Snowflake Man, locals continued to ridicule him, saying snow in Vermont was as common as dirt. In 1931, at the age of sixty-six, Bentley died a poor man, but as he was known to say, "rich with satisfaction." His obituary appeared in many newspapers across the country, and even his own hometown newspaper finally gave him his due. "He saw something in the snowflakes, which other men failed to see. Not because they could not see, but because they had not the patience and understanding to look. Truly, greatness blooms in quiet corners ..."

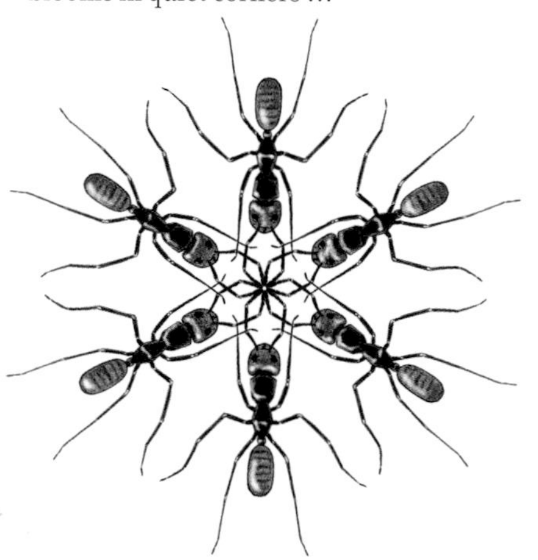

the-century coins in the boys' room. I even cracked their secret code for a long and happy marriage when I started to find their love letters to each other everywhere, some of them written just before Daddy sickened and died. He had even written a love note to my mother in black marker on the inside bottom of the drawer of her nightstand: "You are the love of my life forever"—a touch of sweetness, a reminder, a kiss before bed every night. His notes on the back of the breadbox and on the side of the refrigerator said, "The best thing you can give your children is to love their mother."

Eventually my older sister insisted it was high time I had some company. I'd had company one precious night earlier while "hunting" until 4 a.m. with my younger brother, discovering old letters, looking through old photographs, prying open dusty trunks. And like errant kids again, we left messes everywhere, going from room to room without anyone saying, "Pick up after yourselves," "Finish what you've already started," "Put your things away before you leave."

When my sister arrived, we got busy together, sorting and crying all over again. She tackled the rag drawer in the hallway, the linen closet, and the bedding stored downstairs in a hollowed-out TV console that my father had converted into a "cedar chest" for linens. I pointed out Momma's love of hexagons, and we marveled at our deepening knowledge of who she was. We found letters our parents had exchanged before they were married. We counted all the money they'd left for us and divided it into equal piles. Eventually we voted to spend the money maintaining their home indefinitely as a place where our memories could live on forever. To that end, we had a work party on my birthday and planted their garden with squash, potatoes, cucumbers, tomatoes, beans—all of it. My brother vowed to tend and harvest it.

After a few days, my sister awoke early to pack her car before heading home. Still in my bathrobe, actually my mother's robe, I heard my sister call from the back door, "Sis, come out here. There's something weird going on." I followed her to the driveway as she pointed ahead to what looked like hundreds of immobile black spiders. As I bent down to see why they weren't moving, I realized the driveway was covered in little ants grouped together, head to head, in groups of six.

I have yet to locate an entomologist for a "scientific" explanation of why the ants were in hexagonal huddles. Pep rally? Coffee klatch? It doesn't matter. I like to think it was just another hexagonal wonderment, ranking right up there with my mother's hexagon crocheted scarves, dishcloths, coverlets, etc. Her symbol. Her love. Her brand of harmony.

Here is her pattern for a hexagonal medallion that can be made large or small depending on the size yarn and hook you use. Her one pattern translates easily into knotted creations from bedspreads to dishcloths. But beware. Her medallion has magical powers ...

PROJECT	SIZE	TYPE of YARN	NO. of BALLS or YARDS	NO. of HEXAGONS	CROCHET HOOK SIZE
DISHCLOTH (15" hexagon)	15" x 15"	4-ply 100% Crochet Cotton Thread	1 ball	1	G/6 (4.25 mm)
PILLOW (5" hexagons)	12" x 12"	No. 20 Crochet Cotton Thread	1 ball	7	Size 10 (1.30 mm)
SCARF (5" hexagons)	12" x 52"	No. 20 Crochet Cotton Thread	2 balls	34	Size 10 (1.30 mm)
BEDSPREAD (7" hexagons)	Single 85" x 116"	No. 10 Crochet Cotton Thread	15,000 yards	297	Size 3 (2.10 mm)
	Double 97" x 116"		17,100 yards	341	
	Queen 103" x 121"		19,000 yards	380	
	King 121" x 121"		22,500 yards	449	

Making a Hexagon

(If you're just learnin' to crochet or need a refresher, see my crochet primer on page 118.)

Rnd 1: Ch 6, join with a sl st into a ring, ch 4, 2 tr into ring, work *ch 5, 3 tr in ring, repeat from * 4 more times, ch 5, sl st in top st of first ch-4 at beginning of round.

Rnd 2: Ch 4, 1 tr in each of next 2 tr, *ch 3, 5 tr in center st of next ch-5 loop, ch 3, 1 tr in each of next 3 tr, repeat from * around, end with ch 3, sl st in top st of first ch-4 of round.

Rnd 3: Ch 4, 1 tr in each of next 2 tr, *ch 3, skip next ch-3 loop, 1 sc in next tr, work [ch 4 and 1 sc] in each of next 4 tr, ch 3, skip next chain loop, 1 tr in each of next 3 tr, repeat from * around, end as last round.

Rnd 4: Ch 4, 1 tr in each of next 2 tr, *ch 5, skip next chain loop, 1 sc in next ch-4 loop, work [ch 4 and 1 sc] in each of next 3 chain loops, ch 5, skip next chain loop, 1 tr in each of next 3 tr, repeat from * around, end with ch 5, sl st in top st of first ch-4 of round.

Rnd 5: Ch 4, 1 tr in same st as last sl st, 2 tr in each of next 2 tr, *ch 5, skip next chain loop, 1 sc in next chain loop, work [ch 4 and 1 sc] in each of next 2 chain loops, ch 5, skip next chain loop, 2 tr in each of next 3 tr, repeat from * around, end as last round.

Rnd 6: Ch 4, 1 tr in each of next 2 tr, ch 5, 1 tr in each of next 3 tr, * ch 6, skip next chain loop, 1 sc in next ch-4 loop, ch 4, 1 sc in next chain loop, ch 6, skip next chain loop, 1 tr in each of next 3 tr, ch 5, 1 tr in each of next 3 tr, repeat from * around, end with ch 6, sl st in top of first ch-4 of round.

Rnd 7: Ch 4, 1 tr in each of next 2 tr, * work [3 tr, ch 5, and 3 tr] in next ch-5 loop, 1 tr in each of next 3 tr, ch 6, skip next chain loop, 1 sc in next ch-4 loop, ch 6, skip next chain loop, 1 tr in each of next 3 tr, repeat from * around, end last repeat with ch 6, skip next chain loop, sl st in top st of first ch-4 of round, fasten off.

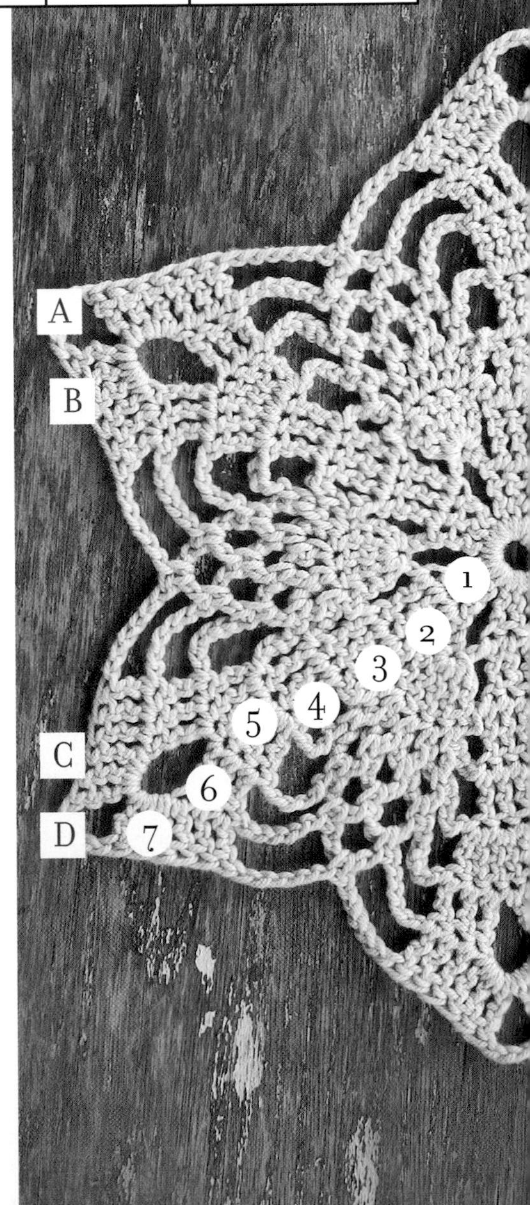

I know everyone loves knitted scarves. *but* if the truth be known, I love crocheted scarves more. (See also the crocheted scarf I made on page 86.) Here's why. I absolutely adore the cozy feeling I get when I have something wrapped around my neck, but crocheted scarves tend to be more light and airy, making them more versatile, and more important, more seasonal. I can wear "cozy" any time of the year, not to mention extra adornment and color.

When it comes to handmade crochet, I've discovered a company you can turn to if you love the look of crochet but haven't the time right now to pick up a hook. Rico Handknits (www.ricohandknits.com) uses 100 percent cotton string in a wide array of colors. For close to twenty years, Rico has been employing women in Thailand who congregate in one home to crochet the day away while the men are at work in the fields. Reminiscent of American quilting bees, the women engage in village chatter while their children play outside or sit in their mother's laps. Husband and wife team Ric and Corinne Fowler have combined their interest in travel and craftsmanship to preserve the traditions and lifestyles of the secluded villagers crocheting and knitting for Rico, keeping families together and flourishing. Since their garments aren't available through mail order, they promise, "Give us a call and we'll help you locate the store nearest you," 1-800-676-7426.

Blocking the Hexagons

Stretch and pin each hexagon to the correct size and shape (see sizes in individual project instructions) on a padded surface. Cover with a damp cloth; press with a warm iron. Remove when dry.

Joining the Hexagons

Using a darning needle and whatever yarn you used in your project, knot yarn around center stitch of a corner ch-5 loop on the first hexagon (see A on illustration, previous page) and sew to corresponding stitch on next hexagon. Sew hexagons together, making loose stitches around the chains on both pieces across to B on illustration; fasten off. Repeat for adjacent corner (from C to D on illustration). Note: It is important not to stitch past the second triple crochet on each corner when joining the individual hexagons. (Sewing past the second triple crochet will cause the work to pucker, keeping it from lying flat.) Hexagons are joined in rows; then rows are joined to one another.

Pillow

Make 7 hexagons. Join into 2 outer rows of 2 hexagons and 1 inner row of 3 hexagons. Hand stitch your finished design onto an 18"-square pillow (velvet works beautifully). Or, like on our front cover, simply stitch one 7" bedspread hexagon onto the front of a 9–12" pillow.

Scarf

Make 34 hexagons. This scarf uses 3 rows of hexagons: 2 outer rows of 11 hexagons and 1 inner row of 12 hexagons.

Bedspread

Single: Make 297 hexagons. Alternate and join 11 rows of 14 with 11 rows of 13.

Double: Make 341 hexagons. Alternate and join 11 rows of 16 with 11 rows of 15.

Queen: Make 380 hexagons. Alternate and join 12 rows of 17 with 11 rows of 16.

King: Make 449 hexagons. Alternate and join 12 rows of 20 with 11 rows of 19.

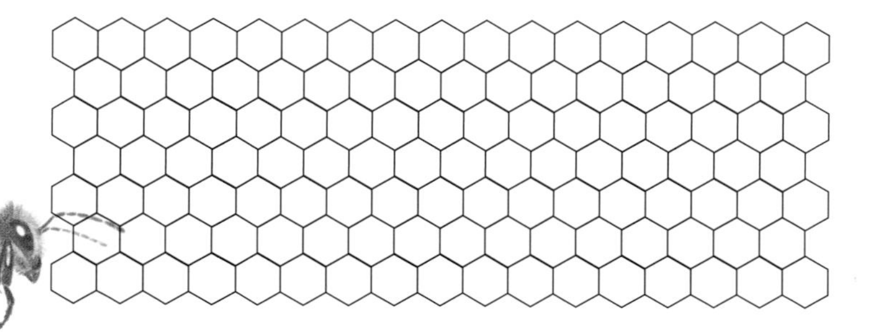

Farmgirl *Beaded Bracelet*

If you're just learnin' to crochet or need a refresher, see my crochet primer on page 118.

Supply List

1 skein (12 yards) Brazilian embroidery floss, 100% rayon
40 beads that will fit onto the rayon thread
1/3 yard 1 1/2"-wide velvet ribbon
1 spool all-purpose sewing thread
Size G/6 (4.25 mm) crochet hook
2 or 3 small sew-on snaps
*The instructions are for a small bracelet, to fit snugly on a wrist with a circumference of about 6". For every 3/4" larger, add an extra 5 chains to your foundation chain.

Instructions

Thread all the beads on the rayon thread. Ch 32.
Row 1: Sc into second ch from hook, *ch 5, skip 4 ch, work a picot (1 sl st, 3 ch, 1 sl st) into the next ch. After you make the first ch of the picot, slide a bead up against your hook so it gets worked into the next sl st. Repeat from * to the end of the row. Turn.
Row 2: *Ch 5, work a picot into third ch of the first 5-ch arch (remember the bead), repeat from * to the last 2 sts of previous row, dc into sc of previous row, sk tch. Turn.
Row 3: Ch 1, sc into first st, *ch 5, work a picot into third ch of the first 5-ch arch (don't forget to slide a bead up to the hook after the first ch of the picot), repeat from * to end. Turn.
Row 4: Repeat Row 2.
Fasten off.

Assembly

1. Measure snugly but comfortably around your wrist. Add 2" to this measurement and cut your ribbon to this length.
2. Turn under one raw edge of the ribbon a scant 1/2" twice and stitch in place by hand with tiny, invisible stitches. Repeat with the other raw edge.
3. Sew the male half of the snaps to the right side of the ribbon, near the edge that is folded under. (It works to use two snaps, but three makes it even more secure.) Fold the other end of the ribbon over the snaps and mark where you want the female halves to go on the wrong side of the bracelet near the other folded edge. Sew them on as well.
4. Snap the ends of the ribbon together and note what part of the ribbon is covered up. When you sew the crochet to the ribbon, you don't want it to be covered up by the ribbon overlapping the crochet.
5. Pin the crochet to the ribbon so it covers as much of the length and width of the ribbon as possible without making the ribbon pucker. Pin in place and stitch on by hand with tiny, invisible stitches.

Acorn Necklace

If you have an old sheer scarf and a handful of smallish objects hanging around, you can make yourself a trendy necklace or belt. (Even old nylons will work!) Sew the scarf into a long, narrow tube, anywhere from about 2–4" wide and as long as you want (you might have to cut your scarf into narrow strips to start with). Start by tying a knot at one end of your tube. You can leave a little bit of loose scarf hanging for decoration if you want. Next, slide a "topless" acorn or a nut, a couple of vintage buttons, or a marble into your tube. Tie another knot close to the object, and repeat until your scarf tube is full. You can put the objects close together or space them farther apart. If you have beads that don't match anything else (left over from random projects or replacements that came with a long-gone beaded sweater), toss them in a bowl, mix them up, and dump about 1 1/2 teaspoons into each space between the knots in place of a single object.

Farmgirl

If you're just learnin' to crochet or need a refresher, see my crochet primer on page 118.

Gauge: 4" x 4" = 13 stitches and 6 rows worked in dc for both

Special abbreviations:
For 2cdc (2-crossed double crochet), skip 1 st, 1 dc into next st, 1 dc into skipped st, working over previous dc.

Hat Supply List

Main Color (MC):
1 skein Lion Brand Moonlight Mohair (bulky specialty) yarn, Purple Mountains, or similar style yarn of your choice
Constrasting Color (CC):
40 yards contrasting color of similar type and weight for trim and flowers
Size H/8 (5 mm) crochet hook
Blunt-tip needle to weave in ends

Hat Instructions

Ch 4 with MC, join chain with a sl st to form a ring.
Rnd 1: Ch 3 (counts as 1 dc), work 11 dc into ring, join with sl st to top of ch (12 dc).
Rnd 2: Ch 3 (for height only, doesn't count as dc), work 2 dc into each st to end of rnd, join with sl st to top of ch (24 dc).
Rnd 3: Ch 3 (doesn't count as dc), dc into first dc, work 2 dc into next dc, *dc in next dc, work 2 dc in next dc*, repeat from * to * to end of rnd, join with sl st to top of dc (36 dc).
Rnd 4: Ch 3 (doesn't count as dc), dc into each of first 2 dc, work 2 dc into next dc, *dc in each of next 2 dc, work 2 dc in next dc*, repeat from * to * to end of rnd, join with sl st to top of ch (48 dc).
Rnd 5: Ch 3 (doesn't count as dc), dc into each of first 3 dc, work 2 dc into next dc, *dc into each of next 3 dc, work 2 dc in next dc*; repeat from * to * to end of rnd, join with sl st to top of ch (60 dc).
Rnds 6 & 7: Ch 3 (doesn't count as dc), dc in each dc, join with sl st to top of ch.
Rnd 8: Ch 3 (doesn't count as dc), *work 2cdc over next 2 st*, repeat from * to * to end of rnd, join with sl st to top of ch.
Rnds 9 & 10: Repeat Rnds 6 & 7.
Rnd 11: Repeat Rnd 8.
Rnds 12 & 13: Repeat Rnds 6 & 7.
Fasten off.

Edging:

With CC, attach yarn to center back edge of hat where rnds are joined. *sk 2 dc, work 5 dc into next dc, sk 2 dc, sc in next dc, sk 1 dc, work 3 dc in next dc, sk 1 dc, sc in next dc*; repeat from * to * around. Fasten off.

Purse Supply List

Main Color (MC):

2	skeins Lion Brand Moonlight Mohair (bulky specialty) yarn, Purple Mountains, or similar style yarn of your choice

Contrasting Color (CC):

40	yards contrasting color of similar type and weight for trim and flowers
1/4	yard fabric for lining
1	spool all-purpose sewing thread to match MC

Size H/8 (5mm) crochet hook

Blunt-tip needle to weave in ends

Flower:

With CC, ch 5. Join ch with sl st to form ring.

Rnd 1: Ch 1 (counts as 1 sc), work 15 sc into ring, join with sl st to ch (16 sc).

Rnd 2: *Ch 3, work 2 dc into each of next 2 sc, ch 3, work sl st into next sc*, repeat from * to * to end of round. Fasten off.

(Note: Flowers can be worked with *ch 4, work 2 tr in each of next 2 sc, ch 4, work sl st into next sc* pattern as well).

Purse Instructions

Front, back, and bottom piece:

Ch 28.

Row 1: Dc in fourth ch from hook, dc in each ch after. Turn.

Rows 2–33: Ch 3, dc in each st. Turn.

Fasten off.

Side pieces (make 2):

Ch 13.

Row 1: Dc in fourth ch from hook, dc in each ch after. Turn.

Rows 2–16: Ch 3, dc in each st. Turn.

Fasten off.

Assembly:

1. Before you assemble your crocheted pieces, lay them out on the lining fabric and trace, leaving a 5/8" seam allowance. Cut these out and set them aside.
2. The short ends of the "front, back, and bottom piece" are the top of the purse, where the handles will be attached. One short end of the side pieces is the top (which will be flush with the top of the other piece), the other short end is the bottom. Find the center of the "front, back, and bottom piece" by folding it in half so the short edges meet each other. Mark the middle on either edge with pins. Find the middle on the bottom of the side pieces by folding the long edges in half to meet each other. Mark the middle of the bottom with a pin on each piece.
3. With the right sides of the crochet out, match up the middle of the bottom of a side piece with the middle of one edge of the "front, back, and bottom piece" and pin together. Starting from the middle, pin

the pieces together all the way up the sides to the top. Ease in fullness around the corners, and match up the rows on the sides. Repeat with the other side.

4. One one end, attach MC yarn with a sl st to top of purse where "front, back, and bottom piece" meets one side piece, and crochet a row of sc through both layers of crochet. Repeat with the other end.

5. Assemble the lining in the same way as the crocheted pieces, either sewing the fabric together by hand or by machine. Place the lining in the purse and fold the top raw edge down about 1" or so below the top of the purse. If you fold the raw edge to the inside of the purse where it will be sandwiched between the crochet and the lining, the raw edge will not be visible or fray. Remove the lining, press the top edge, put the lining back in the purse, and stitch in place with a needle and thread.

Edging:

With CC, attach yarn to one edge of top of purse, preferably where one side meets the front, with a sc. *Sk 2 sts, work 5 dc into next st, sk 2 sts, work 1 sc in next st, sk 1 st, work 3 dc in next dc, sk 1 st, work 1 sc in next st*, Repeat from * to * around. Fasten off.

Handles:

Row 1: With MC, attach yarn to either the front or the back of the purse about 1 1/2" in from the corner and right below the edging with a sc. Sc three more sts into the purse. Turn. This is the base for one handle (and also Row 1).

Rows 2-30: Ch 3. Sk first st and dc into each st after. Turn. On the same front/back side as you started and about 1 1/2" from the opposite corner, sl st the handle to the purse through each dc right below the edging (it should look very similar to the start of your handle). Cut yarn, leaving a 4" tail, and pull through the last loop on hook to tighten. Repeat steps on the other front/back side. Fasten off.

Embellishment:

Make flowers out of CC that are the same as the ones in the hat instructions. Affix one or two to the front of your purse wherever you wish. You could also embellish with buttons or ribbon bows—be creative!

Use your favorite farmgirl hankies and scarves to replace a traditional watchband. The metal spindles that attach the watchband to the watch are very similar to a spring-loaded toilet paper holder. Remove the watchband by releasing the spindles—catch the tiny lip near the end of each spindle with the edge of a pocket knife and pull toward the center. Remove the old band, then reattach the spindles and weave your fabric through them.

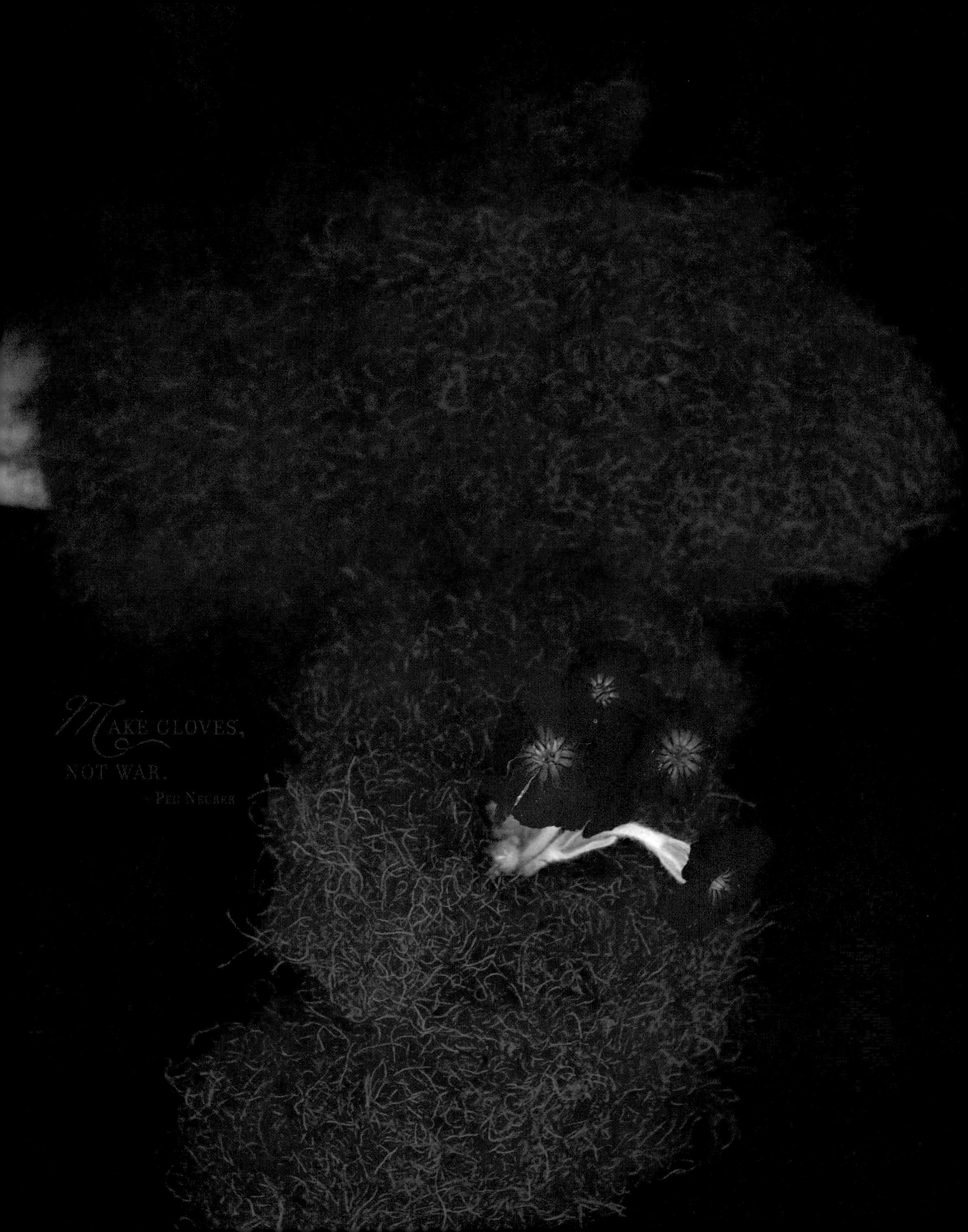

MAKE GLOVES,
NOT WAR.

– PEG NEUBER

Sleighride Mittens

If you're just learnin' to crochet or need a refresher, see my crochet primer on page 118.

Supply List

3 skeins Patons Allure (bulky specialty) yarn, Garnet, or similar style yarn of your choice
Size H/8 (5 mm) crochet hook
Blunt-tip needle for working in ends
Gauge: 4" x 4" = 16 stitches and 4 rows worked in half double crochet

Instructions

Thumbs:

Ch 3 loosely, join chain with a sl st to form a ring.
Rnd 1: Ch 2 (counts as hdc), 5 hdc into loop (6 hdc total). Join with sl st into ch 2.
Rnd 2: Ch 2 (doesn't count as hdc), *hdc into first 2 sts, 2 hdc into next st,* repeat from * to * until end of rnd (8 hdc total). Join with sl st.
Rnd 3: Ch 2 (doesn't count as hdc), hdc into each st to end of rnd, join with sl st. Repeat Rnd 3 until thumb measures 3" long (or as long as you need it). Fasten off.
Repeat this pattern to make a second thumb.

Mitten Hands:

Ch 3 loosely, join chain with a sl st to form a ring.
Rnd 1: Ch 2 (counts as hdc), 5 hdc into ring (6 hdc total). Join with sl st into ch 2.
Rnd 2: Ch 2 (doesn't count as hdc), *hdc into first st, 2 hdc into next st,* repeat from * to * to end of rnd (9 hdc total). Join with sl st.
Rnd 3: Ch 2 (doesn't count as hdc), *hdc into first 2 sts, 2 hdc into next st,* repeat from * to * to end of rnd (12 hdc total). Join with sl st.
Rnd 4: Ch 2 (doesn't count as hdc). *hdc into first 3 sts, 2 hdc into next st,* repeat from * to * to end of rnd (15 hdc total). Join with sl st.
Rnd 5: Ch 2 (doesn't count as hdc), *hdc into first 4 sts, 2 hdc into next st,* repeat from * to * to end of rnd (18 hdc total). Join with sl st.
Rnd 6: Ch 2 (doesn't count as hdc), hdc into each st to end of round. Join with sl st. Repeat Rnd 6 until mitten measures 5 1/2" in length (or as long as you need it—you can try it on at this point to fit).

Attaching Thumb and Remainder of Mitten:

On next rnd, ch 2 (doesn't count as hdc) and work 1 hdc into first st of hand, hdc into each of next 6 hdc of thumb, sk 2 hdc on thumb and 2 hdc on hand, hdc into each of next 15 sts on hand (22 hdc total). Join with sl st.
Next Rnd: Ch 2 (doesn't count as hdc), hdc into each st to end of rnd, join with sl st. Repeat this round until mitten measures 10" in length (you can decrease evenly around on the last few rounds to make a tighter-fitting wrist if desired).

Dress Up Socks & Gloves

Do you remember that pair of gloves you had to buy at the gas station last winter when the weather was so bad your windshield wipers were frozen to your windshield? Turn them into a cute new accessory. Simply use silk ribbon in varying widths to embroider a lazy daisy, a snowflake, or just a few colorful stripes. Or gussy up a pair of anklet socks: Crochet a bit of trim right onto the edge of your socks. Use #10 thread and a #12 (.75mm) steel crochet hook (those are the really little kind).

Row 1: Sc 5 into edge of sock, 2 picots, and repeat until you've gone all the way around the sock.
Row 2: Starting at the right of picots in fourth st, ch 3, sk 2 sts, dc in next st, *ch 9, sk 1 st at left of picots, dc in next st, sk 2 sts, dc in next st; rep from * until you complete the round.
Row 3: 5 sc, 3 picots, 5 sc around every 9-ch space. Repeat for all of them.

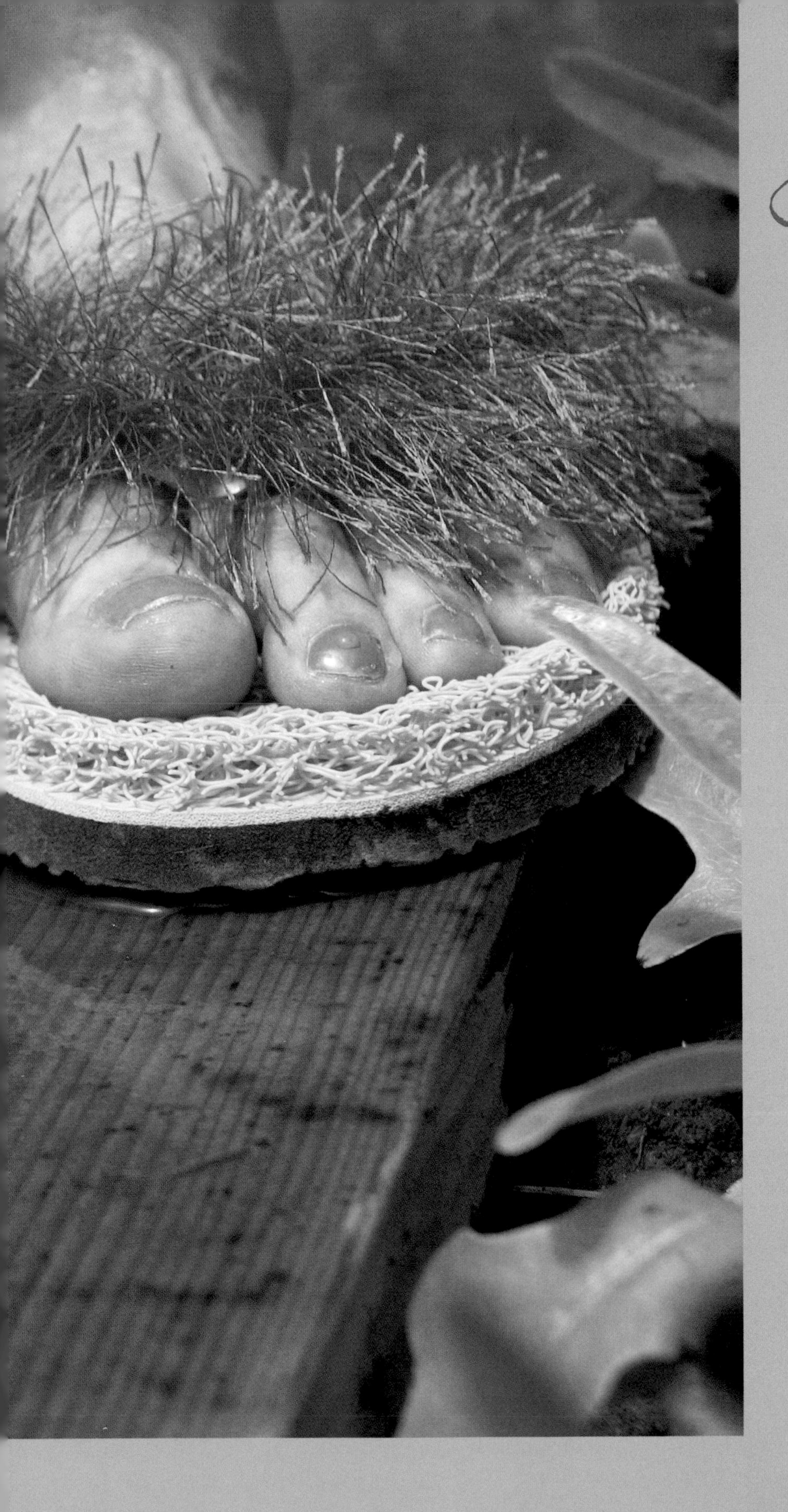

Crocheted *Flip-flops*

If you're just learnin' to crochet or need a refresher, see my crochet primer on page 118.

Supply List

1 skein Lion Brand Fun Fur (bulky specialty) yarn or similar style yarn of your choice
1 pair flip-flops with narrow rubber straps that contrast with the yarn
Size K/10.5 (6.5 mm) crochet hook

*For fuzzier flip-flops, crochet with two strands of yarn instead of one. You don't need to buy two skeins; just unwrap one end from the outside and gently tug the other end out from the middle of the skein.

Instructions

1. Start with a slip knot on your hook. Slip stitch around the rubber strap on one of your flip-flops like this: slide the hook under the strap, yarn over, and pull the hook under strap and through the loop on the hook. Repeat until one side of your flip-flop is done. (It is easiest to crochet one side of the flip-flop and then cut the yarn and start fresh on the other side of the toe piece.)
2. Squish the yarn already on your flip-flop to make it really fluffy and create room for more crochet; otherwise it will look limp.
3. When you fill up your flip-flop, just fasten off as usual. Repeat with the second flip-flop.

Ever wondered what to do with those worn-out beaded sweaters you come across in second-hand stores?

Cut a portion off and stitch it into an evening purse; then make a handle out of some faux pearls.

Accessorize your Rose Garden Scarf with a patched jacket ...

When you find a wool jacket that wasn't kept safe from moths, turn it into an opportunity to show off your creative mending abilities. Patches that look like patches are farmgirl handiwork at its braggin' best!

Rose Garden Scarf

Just learnin' to crochet or need a refresher? See my crochet primer—everything from positioning your hands, to basic and more complicated stitches, to attaching pieces together—complete with both photos and drawings, starting on page 118.

Special stitches:
Fptr (front post triple crochet): Yo twice, insert hook from front to back, then to front (going around the "post" or vertical part of the stitch), draw up a loop (yo and draw through 2 loops on hook) 3 times. Skip st behind fptr.

Bptr (back post triple crochet): Yo twice, insert hook from back to front, then to back (going around the "post" or vertical part of the stitch), draw up a loop (yo and draw through 2 loops on hook) 3 times. Skip st behind bptr.

Supply List

3 skeins Cascade Malizia (bulky specialty) yarn, Color 10, or similar style yarn of your choice
Size N/13 (9 mm) crochet hook
Blunt-tip needle for finishing

Instructions

Cut 36 pieces of yarn 14" long for fringe and set aside.
Ch 14. Turn.
Row 1: Tr in fifth ch from hook and in each ch after that. Turn.
Row 2: Ch 4, fptr around each tr post. Turn.
Row 3: Ch 4, bptr around each tr post. Turn.
Repeat Rows 2 and 3 alternately until scarf is desired length or yarn is gone.
Fasten off.

Fringe

Loop two strands of the yarn you set aside over your crochet hook. Line up the ends so the yarn is folded evenly in half. Stick your hook through the corner of one end of the scarf and pull the fold through. Pull ends of yarn through this loop and pull to tighten fringe. Repeat along both ends of the scarf with the remaining yarn.

ROSEBUD DISH SCRUBBIES

Supply List

10 yards nylon netting (enough for 12 scrubbies)
Size J/10 (6 mm) crochet hook

Instructions

Cut netting into 3" strips (3" x 10 yards) and wind into balls. It takes 2 strips to make 1 scrubbie, with enough left over to stuff the pad.

Ch 6. Join with sl st to form ring.
Rnd 1: Work 2 sc in each ch. Do not join (work in spiral fashion). (12 sc)
Rnd 2: Working in back loops only throughout project, sc in each sc around, increasing 6 sc evenly spaced. (Be careful not to work increases directly over those in the previous round.) (18 sc)
Rnd 3: Sc in each sc around, increasing 6 sc evenly spaced. (24 sc)
Rnd 4: Sc in each sc around, increasing 6 sc evenly spaced. (30 sc)
Rnd 5: Work one round even (sc in each sc around). (30 sc)
Rnd 6: Sc in next 4 sc, decrease 1 sc. Repeat around. (24 sc)
Rnd 7: Sc in each sc around, decreasing 6 sc evenly spaced. (18 sc)
Rnd 8: Sc in each sc around, decreasing 6 sc evenly spaced. (12 sc)

Stuff the scouring pad with scraps of nylon net.

Rnd 9: Sc in each sc around, decreasing 6 sc evenly spaced. (6 sc)

Break off nylon netting and weave in end (I use a darning needle and pull the needle through with a pair of pliers).

Linen Closet *Stitching*

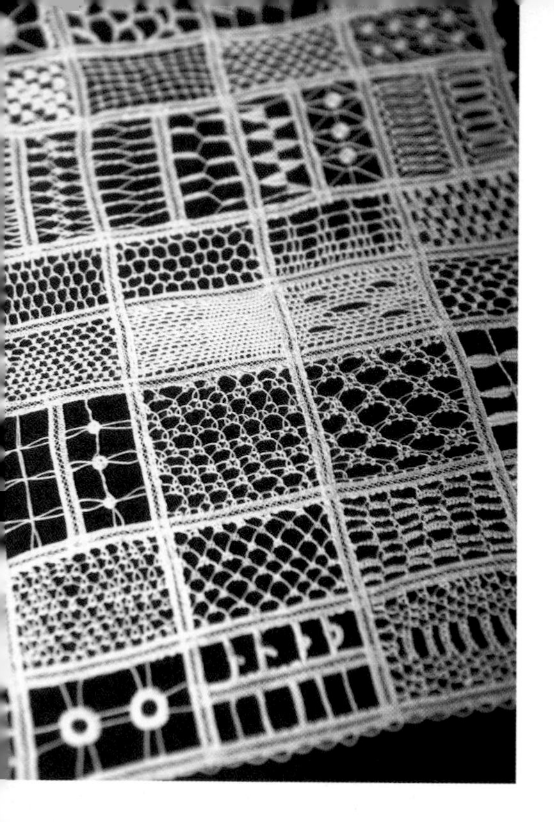

Lace WITH GRACE

The nursery rhyme "One, two, buckle my shoe ..." originated as a way to teach children how to make lace. "Five, six, pick up sticks" refers to the picking up of lacing bobbins.

An old craft that has been the source of untold delicate beauty for the past five hundred years, lace making is being revived in many places, including here in my hometown, Moscow, Idaho.

In 1992, Kathleen Warnick (right) got together with five friends to form the Appaloosa Lace Guild. With a membership that now hovers near thirty, the guild teaches the art of lace making to the next generation on alternate Sundays, year round.

Although lacing looks difficult, Moscow's lacers know their stuff and like to joke that all you really need to "lace" is to be able to count to four and know two moves: a cross and a twist.

Kathleen, who has been lacing since she was a young teenager, is the author of the book *Legacy of Lace*.

"I learned to lace from a book myself," Kathleen pointed out to me when I came with my camera to one of their gatherings. As I watched their hands, it looked to me as if they were doing dot-to-dot, much like the entertainment I remember from my childhood coloring books, using pins as dots and thread instead of a pencil.

That got me to thinking that maybe something as complicated as the art of lace making *can* be handed down through books. (Another project for a future book!)

Lace making requires a firm pillow about the size of a lap desk, as well as a small pinkeeper that can be attached to the pillow to hold the lacer's straight pins. To make the lace, fine thread is wound on finger-sized bobbins that are used as carriers and then crossed and twisted in various combinations to accomplish different stitches.

The number of bobbins you need depends on the complexity of the design—some lace designs require hundreds! The bobbins themselves can be fascinating, and they are made from all sorts of materials: wood, porcelain, glass, bone, pewter, brass inlaid (see page 88). Some antique bobbins are adorned with jewels and beads; others carry inscriptions with romantic sayings hand carved by men for their fiancées as mementos of their marriage proposals.

As I was leaving the Lace Guild's gathering, I promised, "I'll be back."

"Just remember," they warned me, "once you start, you'll never be able to stop!"

Tatting & Chatting

With more and more people wanting to visit my farm, I decided to open it up to tourists and visitors every Fourth of July weekend for a two-day Farm Fair. Each year on Independence Day weekend, about a thousand people find their way up my road for a farm-style celebration that includes things like picnic lunches, homemade strawberry shortcake (topped with real whipped cream!), lots of u-pick vegetables and flowers, fresh-baked bread, a rolling-pin-throwing contest, hopscotch and pony rides for the kids, dancing to live farm-style music, shopping for farm collectibles, and demonstrations that range from growing your own fuel (biodiesel) to tatting and spinning wool from your own sheep.

Why the pilgrimage to a farm? One of last year's visitors grabbed me along my lane to say, "Okay, I've figured out how to have chickens, but I still don't know how to grow anything. How do I plant a seed and have it grow?" On an errand headed elsewhere, I improvised by grabbing a nearby stick, making a furrow and showing her how, using the gravel in my driveway. In five minutes I taught her my "dust mulch" method. (Dust mulch means digging a furrow with your hoe, running water down it, letting the water soak in, planting seeds in the mud, then covering them with a fine dust using the hands as clod sifters and walking along the furrow, heel to toe, pushing the seeds down into the wet soil. Watering from the top after planting a seed creates a hard top crust that is difficult for seedlings to break through.)

Back at home, my "drive-by" visitor wrote to say, "We recently visited your farm. I was the one with *all* the little girls and the baby. Anyway, now I have an interest in using our ten acres for farming. You have been such an inspiration in so many ways. Since reading your magazine, I've even changed my view of environmental issues I thought I knew about, certain political issues, etc. Thanks for your take on things and for taking the time to teach others. Your knowledge shines through as the best kind of food." She signed her note, "Future Farmgirl, Vicki."

Handing down knowledge was always part of a farmer's job. Since most of us are from farm origins (not so very long ago if you stop to think about it), we are beginning to realize that living a more can-do, make-do, farm-frugal lifestyle and knowing how to grow our own food should be included in our bag of tricks, especially since it's getting trickier and trickier to carve out a healthy niche in our modern-day world. It seems like the longer people commute or the longer they spend indoors, the stronger their farm fantasies. Trouble is, as farms vanish from our landscape, so does the farm classroom—the perfect place to learn by doing.

Dear MaryJane,
I'm new to the farmgirl thang. Although I've always been a country girl, it was only recently that I planted my first garden, sewed anything other than attaching a button, or even came up with a creative solution instead of just running to the store to buy whatever it was I was needing. I love your book and just bought a copy for my mother-in-law (a true farmgirl to the core) for her upcoming seventy-third birthday. She will devour it!

Question ... Will there be Pay Dirt Farm School videos available any time soon? I think they were alluded to in the acknowledgment section of the book (yeah, I read *every* page). Coming to Idaho for a week (with two toddlers in tow) is pretty much out of the question, but I really want to learn what you have to teach. Videos would be a great help to me and many other farmgirl newbies.

Keep up the fantastic work!
Jet in Missouri

Dear Jet,
We're working on a series of how-to videos, which will be available by subscription on our website, in addition to a couple of TV specials. Stay tuned!
MaryJane

"You can teach a student a lesson for a day; but if you can teach him to learn by creating curiosity, he will continue the learning process as long as he lives."

—Clay P. Bedford

Katie Saunders, a Moscow, Idaho, native, was fascinated by tatting the first time she saw it. She crocheted, knitted, and loved to sew, but the intricate designs of tatting beckoned her. "So few people knew how, I felt I needed to learn before it died out." A mutual friend introduced her to Gladys Lee, who, at ninety-six years of age, was teaching several other women to tat. She and Katie hit it off right away. Recalls Katie, "It began as a tatting lesson, but I ended up going to visit once a week for four years because I also loved her stories. To me, it was like listening to *Little House on the Prairie*." Katie, nineteen and homeschooled K–12, is currently studying classical ballet at the University of Idaho. An accomplished musician, Katie plays guitar and fiddle and makes music with her seven siblings. She also teaches Irish dance and has been known to demonstrate her love for the dance on the tables of the local coffeehouse.

So for the last eleven years, I've tried to slake a growing collective thirst for agrarian knowledge in a more formal way by creating a school that turns my farm into a hands-on classroom, beyond the knowledge that can be garnered drive-by style.

Here at Pay Dirt Farm School (an official nonprofit organization, www.maryjanesfarm.org/about/paydirt), I've trained just about every kind of would-be farmer, from retired military men to wealthy housewives to a fourteen-year-old farmgirl wannabe. In the beginning, students stayed through a growing season, but over time, teaching taught me something too: how to condense and distill what my parents taught me into a much shorter period of time. Now I can jump-start and launch a future farmer in a mere seven days. And with the number of farms run by women having grown by 86 percent since the early eighties, there is a growing demand for information on how to run a farm more holistically and systematically.

Since our modern-day world seems to value recreation and travel more than wholesome food, farmers are figuring out that by combining the three, farming can pay. The perfect example is a farm bed and breakfast. A farmer can charge upward of $300 per night for a farm stay that includes a farm-fresh breakfast. But selling those same breakfast ingredients at the local farmers' market might bring the farmer $5 at best. And as part of their hands-on farm experience, the guests probably pitched in to help milk the family cow or gather eggs ... selling the good life!

A recent Pay Dirt attendee, an amazing woman named Libbie, drove fourteen hours from Utah for one of my intensive one-week sessions. Her goal? To save a farm that has been in her family since 1875 by converting it to an organically operated agritourism farm.

Libbie decided she wanted to start with a couple of Dexter dairy cows. (Small in size, Dexters are a gentle breed from Ireland that almost became extinct. Farm tourists, in particular, adore them because of their petlike demeanor.)

And her week here? Using a learn-by-doing method, my son, Emil, taught her how to build fences and clean garlic. My husband, Nick, taught her how to become a rototiller mechanic and take care of cows. Julie, our recipe developer, taught her to preserve food. Carol, my graphic designer, taught her how to create farm brochures. I taught her how to take the photos she'd need for her brochures, how to plant and grow things, rehandle tools, keep her tools sharp, and where to buy superior tools with an eye for verticle-grain handles. And run a bed and breakfast. Katy, another Pay Dirt Farm School student that week, taught us all how to tat. Kory, another farmhand, taught her how to keep bees and harvest honey. My daughter, Meg, who answers our phones,

Katy King is the most grounded, accomplished twenty-one-year-old I've met in a long time. Homeschooled her entire life, she spent four years from age eight to twelve helping her father selectively log their twenty wooded acres of land in Washington. She also holds a "distance learning" degree from a liberal arts college, where she earned straight As. Katy taught herself to tat at age fourteen and then began offering tatting classes. During the week she attended our Pay Dirt Farm School, Katy taught us farmgirls how to tat (we already knew how to chat!). Katy says being homeschooled has certainly shaped her ability to interact with all age groups easily. Her best friends range in age from six to eighty-nine! (She considers her three brothers and her parents her very best.) Her other hobbies are gardening, crocheting, knitting, backpacking, fishing, and barn dismantling! Someday she'd like to write a how-to book on turning found or used items into furniture and accessories.

dispensed her passion for our over-the-top customer service. I introduced her to the Zen of chickens, expounding on how I think the chicken (the oldest domesticated animal on earth) and a beehive are examples of the unity and coherence of life—an integral part of the much larger "order of things." Midweek during her stay, we gathered in our historic one-room schoolhouse for swing-dance lessons taught by Anna, our farm seamstress. Libbie spent her last day here with a nearby raw-milk farmer learning how to make her milk and cheese dreams come true.

And then there were all the little unplanned things thrown in as she and I walked about dreaming and dissecting her future: while brandishing dried poppy heads like salt shakers to fill our mouths with the virgin-fresh flavor of poppy seeds, nothing at all like the stale, flavorless, speckled topping found on grocery store buns; or breaking ears of corn from their stalks and eating them raw, the milk running down our chins; or listening closely as the sun was setting and hearing the sigh of overheated plants.

With the farmgirl movement (rural renaissance) now in full swing and demands on my time changing, I'm the dreamer now, coming up with some far-flung ideas like training farmers to train farmers to train farmers. It would involve something I call the exchange economy; similar to keeping in touch with your neighbors by running next door for a cup of sugar, you'd borrow knowledge instead.

Here's an example of how an exchange economy works. When my two children were toddlers, I drove an old 1953 Ford (fix-or-repair-daily) pickup truck. The only gas station in the town of four hundred where I lived was owned and run by two older brothers who looked like the cast from a Norman Rockwell painting. It became my full-service stop. Over the course of two years, with the brothers mentoring me, lending tools, and entertaining my kids, I gradually overhauled my truck. They taught me things like how to rebuild my carburetor, install new king pins, and replace the steering box. In exchange, I gave them regular hair cuts, kept their restroom clean, and organized their tools.

In the neighborhood where I grew up, young mothers, mine included, joined forces for the purpose of giving domestic instruction to their daughters. For years we were schooled on a regular basis, after school, in the basics of stitching, cooking, gardening, home economy, manners, and child rearing. We were divided into lesson groups, with every mother's personality and skills added to the rotation mix.

Whether it's a matter of liability or responsibility, we've turned our teaching and our learning over to expensive institutions. But the very best kind of knowledge is only a chat (or tat) session away.

Reading a Tatting Pattern

Here is a list of abbreviations used in the tatting patterns and instructions on the next few pages:

ds: double stitch
p or "–": picot
R: ring
Ch: chain
j or "+": join
Cl: close (a ring)
Rw: reverse work

For example, a pattern for "Making a Ring" (page 103) would look like this:
R. 5ds, 1p, 5ds, 1p, 5ds, 1p, 5ds, Cl Rw.
Ch. 10ds, Rw.
*R. 5ds, j (to last picot of last ring), 5ds, 1p, 5ds, 1p, 5ds, Cl, Rw.
Ch. 10ds, Rw.*
Repeat from * to * until your work has reached the desired length.

INSTITUTE
UTAH

#3
#5
#7
#8
These are life-size examples of tatting, so use these needle and thread combinations as a guide for your own projects.
Pearl Cotton #5, Needle #3
Crochet Thread Cebelia #10, Needle #5
Pearl Cotton #8, Needle #5
Cordonette Crochet Thread #20, Needle #5
Pearl Cotton #12, Needle #7
Cordonette Crochet Thread #30, Needle #7
Cordonette Crochet Thread #40, Needle #7
Cordonette Crochet Thread #50, Needle #7
Cordonette Crochet Thread #60, Needle #7
Special Dentelles #80, Needle #8
Cordonette Crochet Thread #100, Needle #8

Making a Double Stitch

1. Thread your needle, leaving about 6" of thread for a tail. Look at the threads coming out of the eye of your needle. There should be two lengths of thread: the shorter tail end and the long piece attached to the ball. Pick up the long end a couple of feet away from the eye of the needle. Place the thread behind the needle and hold it in place with your right index finger.

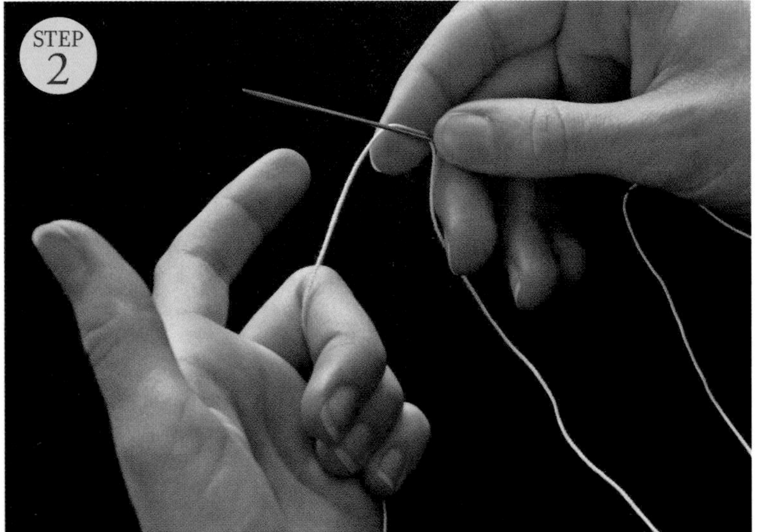

2. Close the bottom three fingers of your left hand around the end of the thread that is attached to the ball.

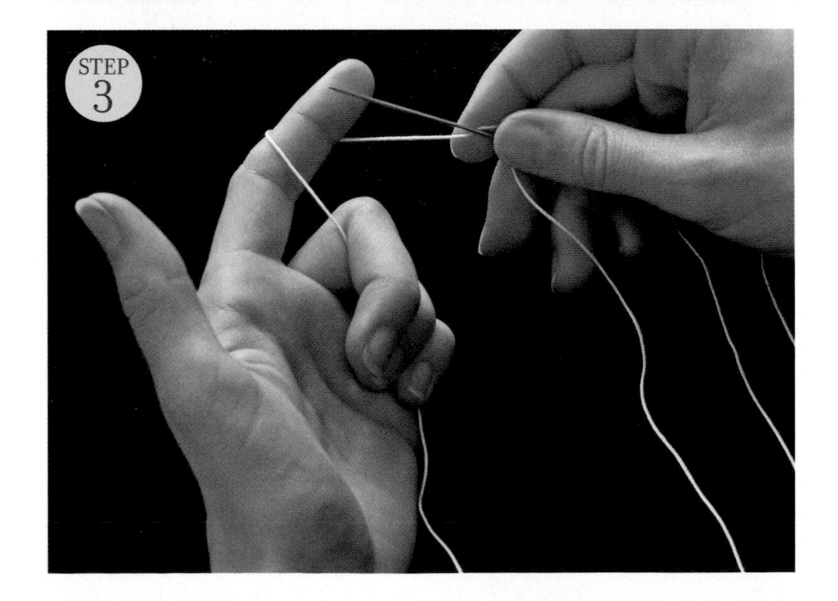

3. Wrap the piece of thread that you're holding in your left hand around your left index finger one time in a clockwise direction.

Making a Double Stitch (continued)

4. Starting from the bottom of your index finger and going upward, slide the needle under the string on your finger. Once the loop of thread around your finger is also around your needle, slide your finger out.

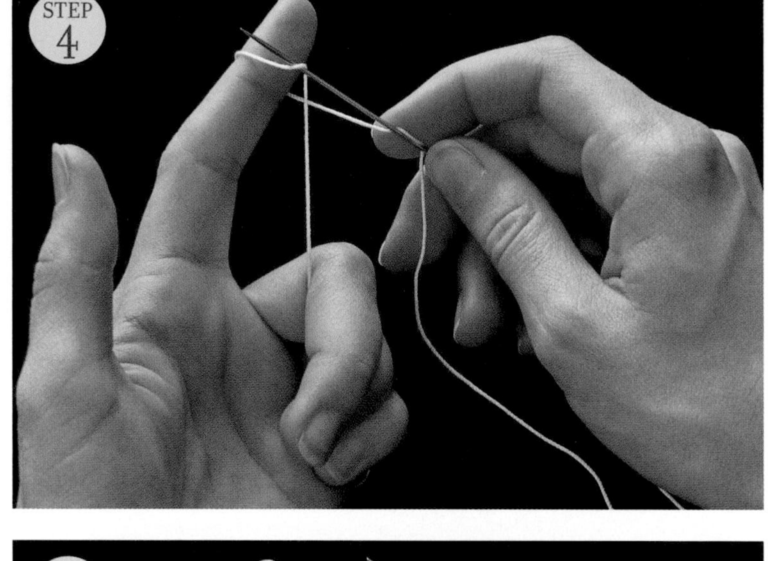

5. Slide this part of the stitch down to your right index finger and hold it in place with that finger. Pull gently on the thread with your left hand to make sure the stitch is snug but not too tight. This is the first half of your double stitch.

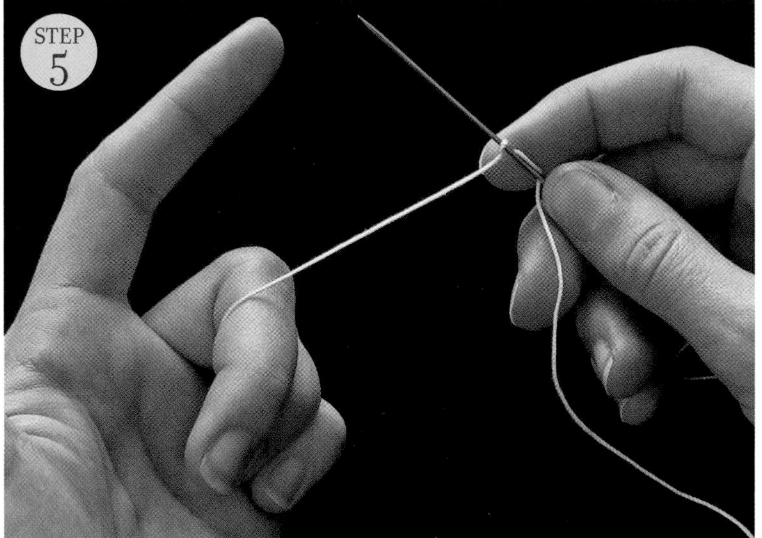

6. Now wrap the thread around your left index finger in a counter-clockwise direction.

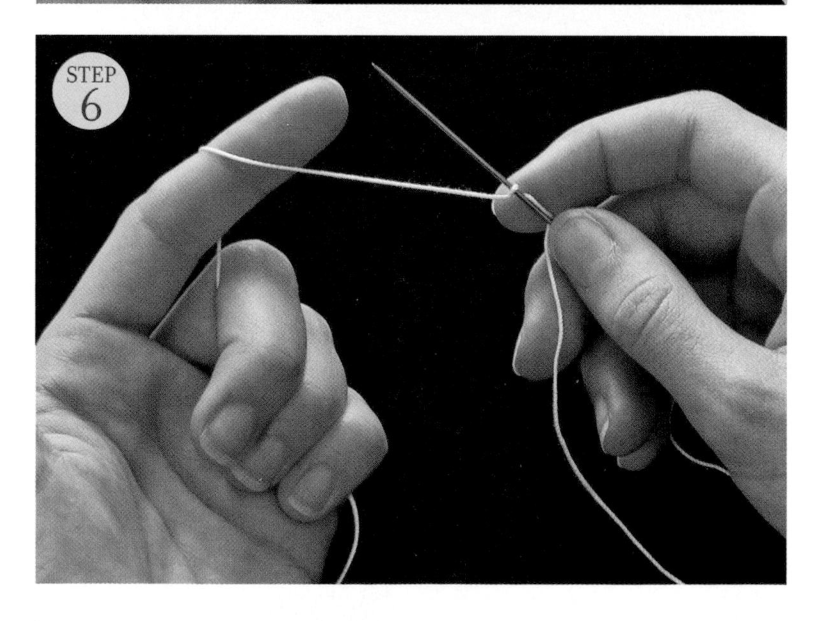

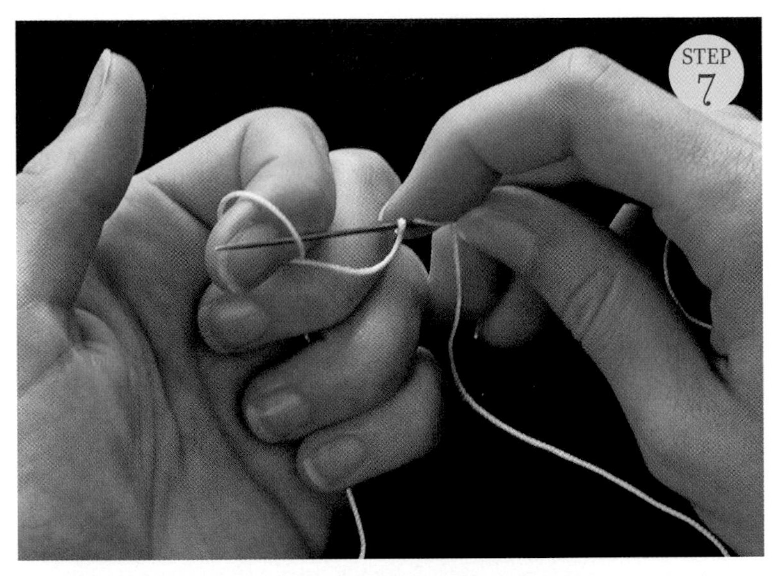

Making a Double Stitch (continued)

7. Bend your left index finger over so you can see your knuckles. Slide the needle under the thread from your knuckle toward your fingernail. Pull your finger out of the loop of thread once it is on your needle. Pull the loop of thread down the needle until it is snug against the other half of the stitch.

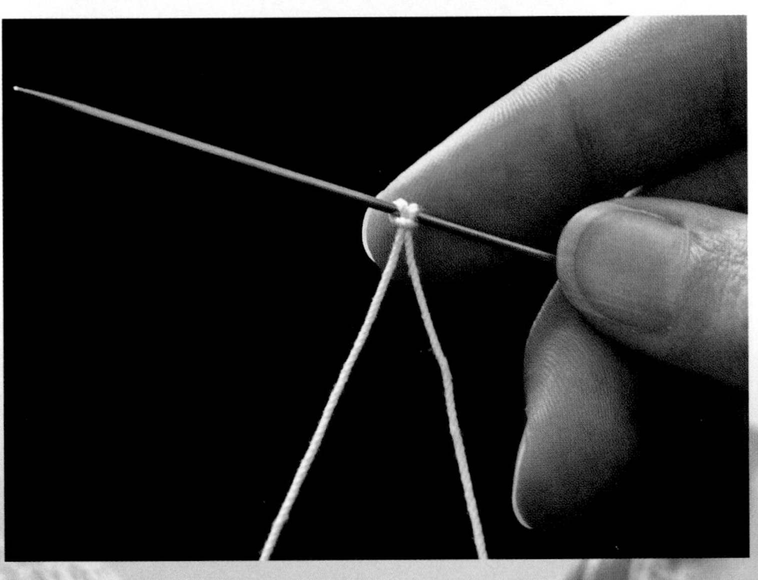

Your double stitch is now complete. This is really the only stitch in tatting; everything else is just a manipulation of the double stitch. Repeat steps 3–7 to create another double stitch. When you are making double stitches one right after the other, slide each stitch snugly against the others. Practice your double stitches until each one is consistent.

Making a Picot

A picot is simply a space of thread left between two double stitches.

1. When your pattern calls for a picot, make the first half of your double stitch. When you're sliding the stitch down the needle, stop it about 1/2" away from the other stitches with your right index finger.

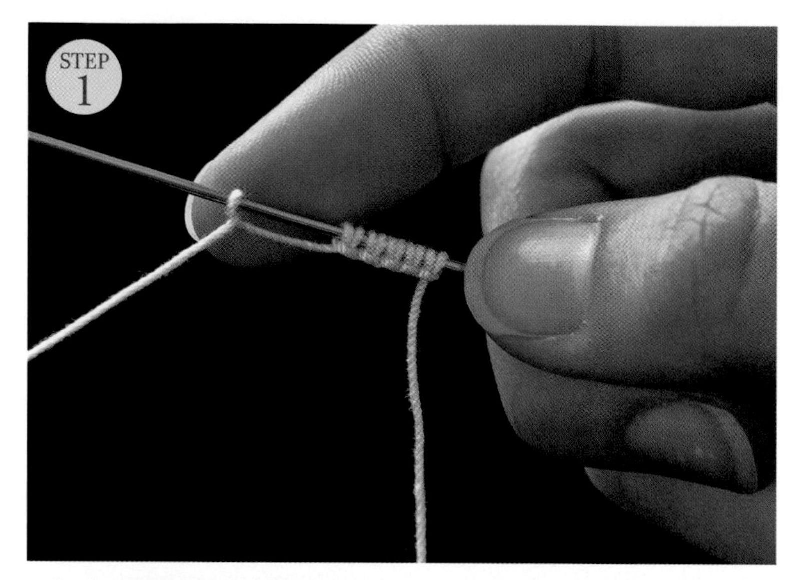

2. Make the second half of your double stitch and slide it down the needle to your first half. Now slide the whole double stitch down to meet the previous ones. There should be a little loop of thread sticking out between this stitch and the one right before it: this loop is your picot. Practice making five double stitches and one picot (and then five more double stitches, etc.) a few times until all of your picots are the same size.

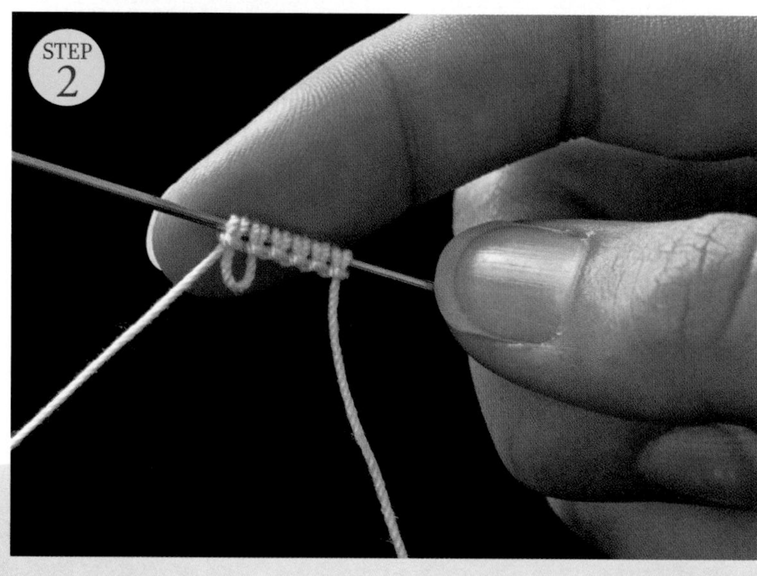

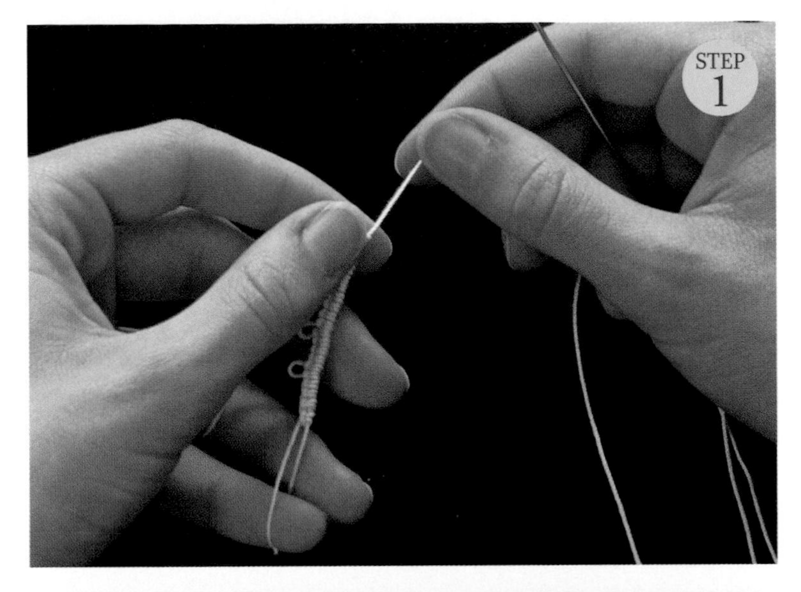

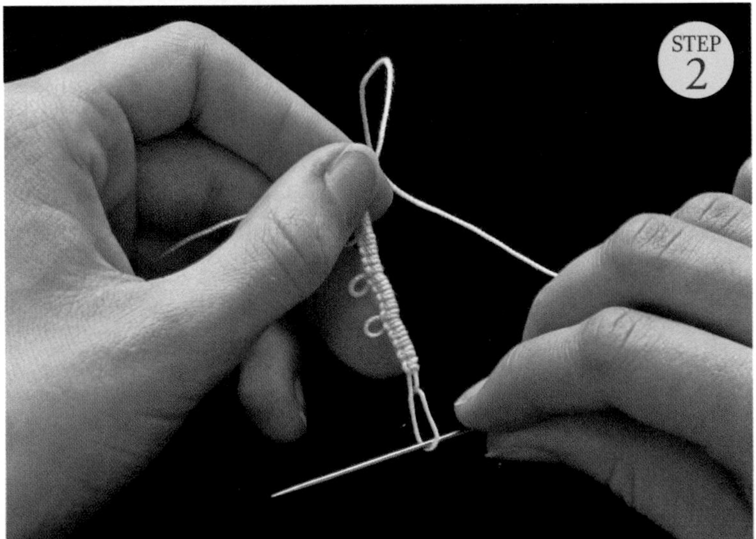

Making a Ring

After you are comfortable with your double stitches and picots, it's time to actually make something out of them!

1. Start by tatting this onto your needle: five double stitches, one picot, five double stitches, one picot, five double stitches, one picot, and five more double stitches. Hold on to the needle with your right hand above the stitches (closer to the pointy end). With your left thumb and index finger, slide the stitches down toward the end of the needle. Carefully slide the stitches off the needle, making sure that you don't let go of the double stitches. Slide your stitches farther down the thread. There is a loop of thread on one end of the stitches; stick your left pinkie finger into the loop to help keep the thread from tangling. Keep pulling on the needle end of the thread. The large loop of thread will get smaller and smaller, and if your finger wasn't in it, it would disappear completely. Don't let that happen!

2. Take your finger out of the loop and bring the needle up through it. Keep pulling on the needle to close up the ring all the way. You've just completed one ring.

This is what your ring looks like after step 2.

Making a Ring
(continued)

3. Flip your ring over from right to left like you're turning the page of a book. This is called reversing the work and should make the threads cross and create a little hole. Bring the needle up through the hole and pull the strings tight to create a knot. This knot will help keep your project together. Also note that the side of the ring that is facing you is the "wrong" side.

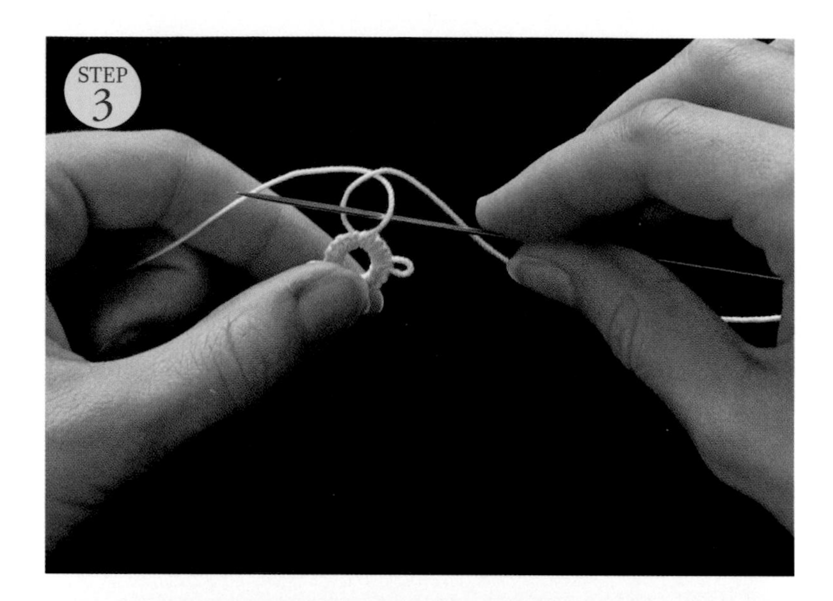

Making a Chain

1. Put your needle on top of the knot you just made. Make ten double stitches on your needle. Make sure that the first one is right next to the ring; it's easy to leave a little space of thread if you're not careful.

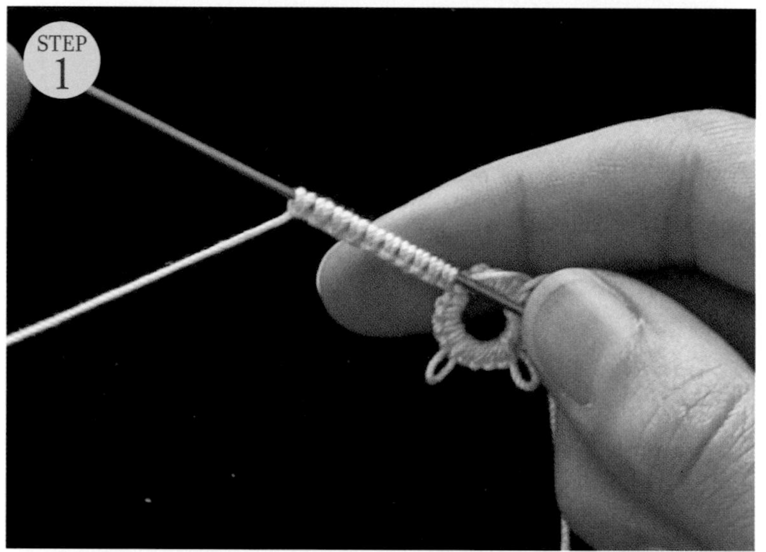

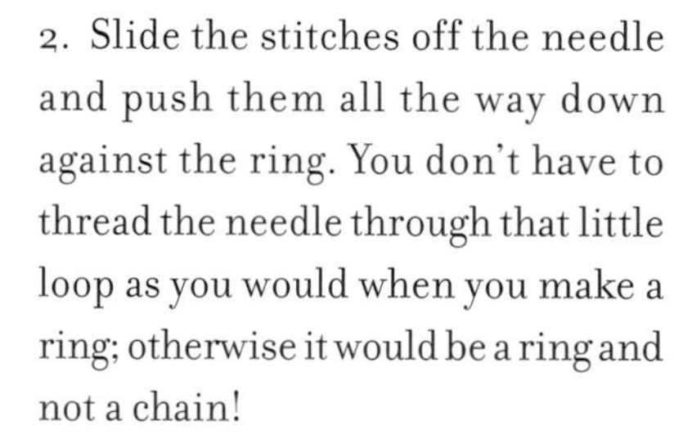

2. Slide the stitches off the needle and push them all the way down against the ring. You don't have to thread the needle through that little loop as you would when you make a ring; otherwise it would be a ring and not a chain!

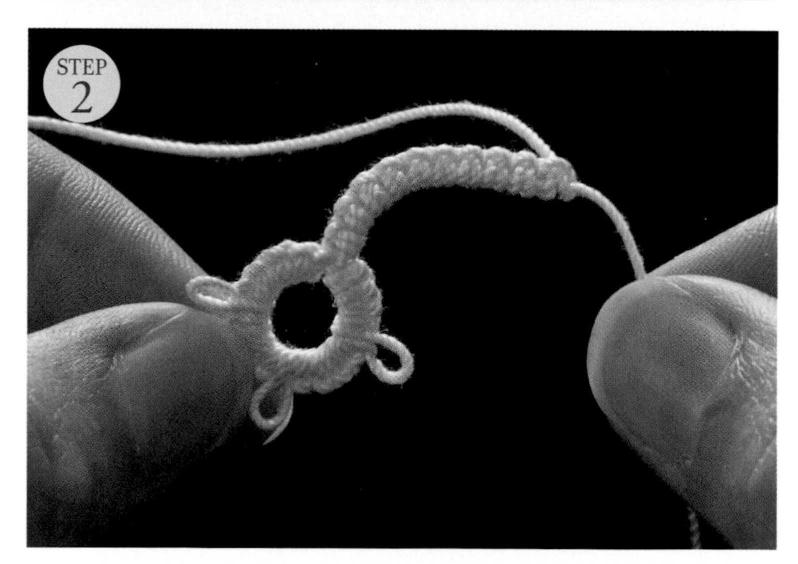

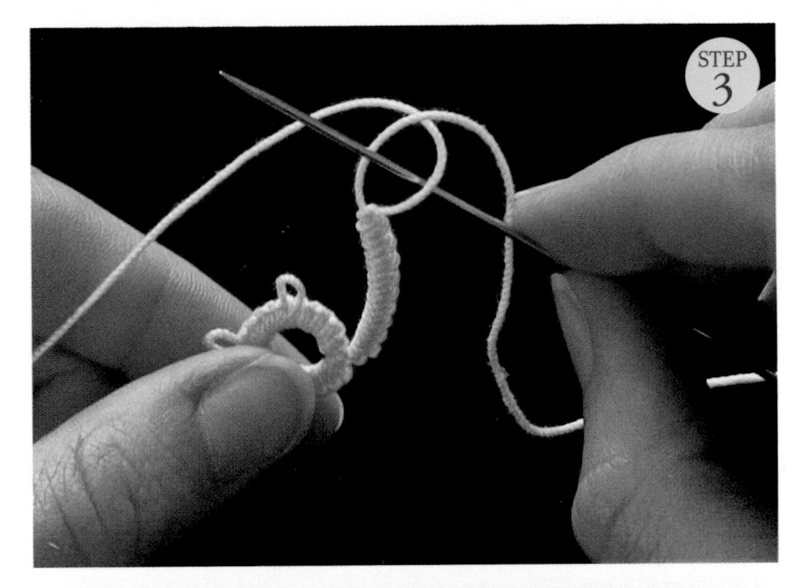

Making a Chain
(continued)

3. Reverse your work by turning it over right to left, like a page in a book. Bring your needle up through the little loop of thread and tie a knot. Your chain is complete!

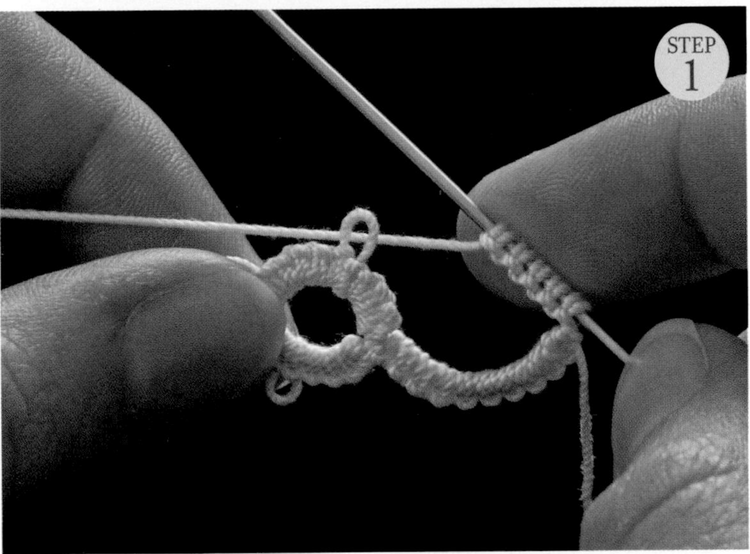

Making the Second Ring and Joining

1. Put five double stitches on your needle. At this point, you would be ready to make another picot, as in the first ring, but you have to attach your new ring to the first ring instead. To do this, start by grasping the thread in your left hand and then place it behind the last picot you made on your first ring.

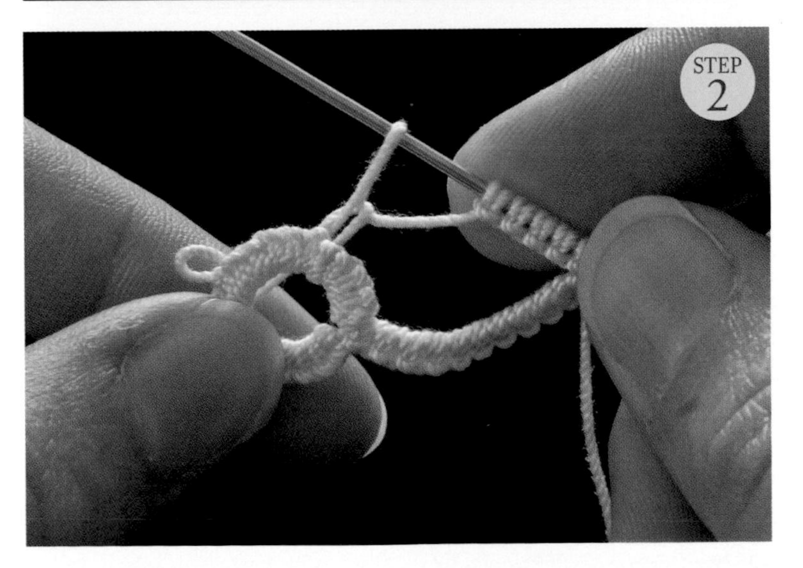

2. Using the tip of your tatting needle or a small crochet hook, pull the thread up through the picot. Note that you're pulling a loop of thread through the picot, not putting the picot on your needle.

Making the Second Ring and Joining
(continued)

3. Slide the thread down the needle to meet the double stitches and pull on the thread so it tightens around the needle. This loop you made around the needle does not count as a part of any double stitch, it is a "join."

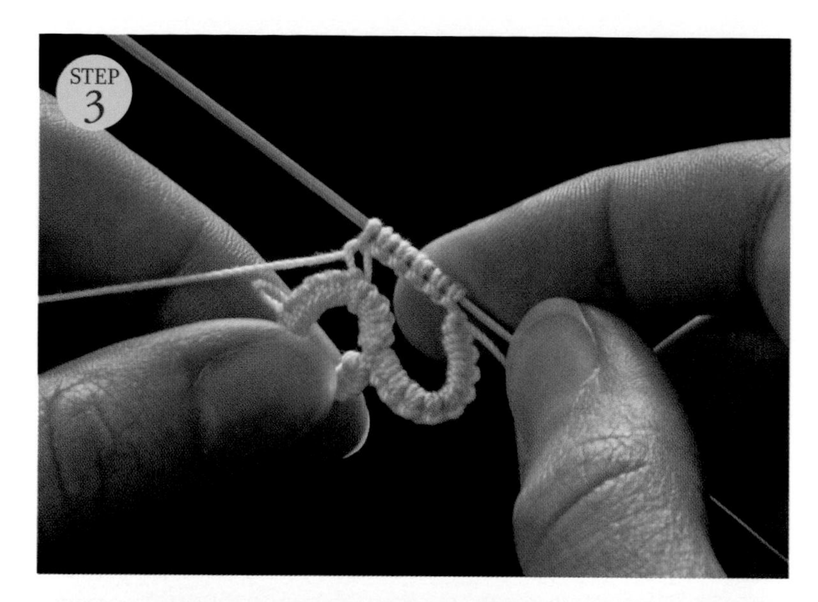

4. Now make five double stitches, one picot, five double stitches, one more picot, and five more double stitches on your needle. Close the ring by sliding the stitches off your needle, but remember the little loop of thread that you have to bring your needle through to complete the ring! Pull the string tight, and reverse the work by turning it over like a page in a book. Reverse the work and tie a knot as in Step 3 of "Making a Ring."

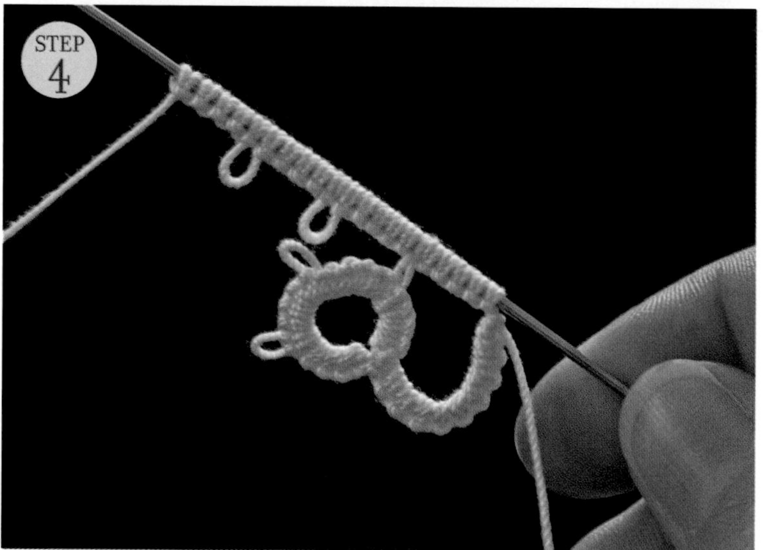

Making the Second Chain

1. Place your needle on top of the ring just as you did for the first chain. Put ten double stitches on your needle. Note how the stitches on your needle look compared to the first chain you made. Slide the stitches off the needle, reverse your work, and don't forget to tie a knot as in Step 3 of "Making a Chain."

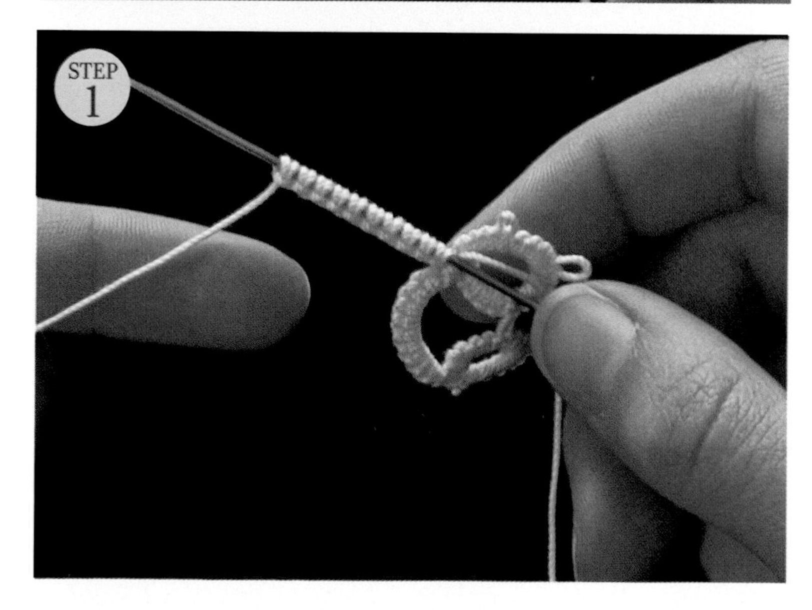

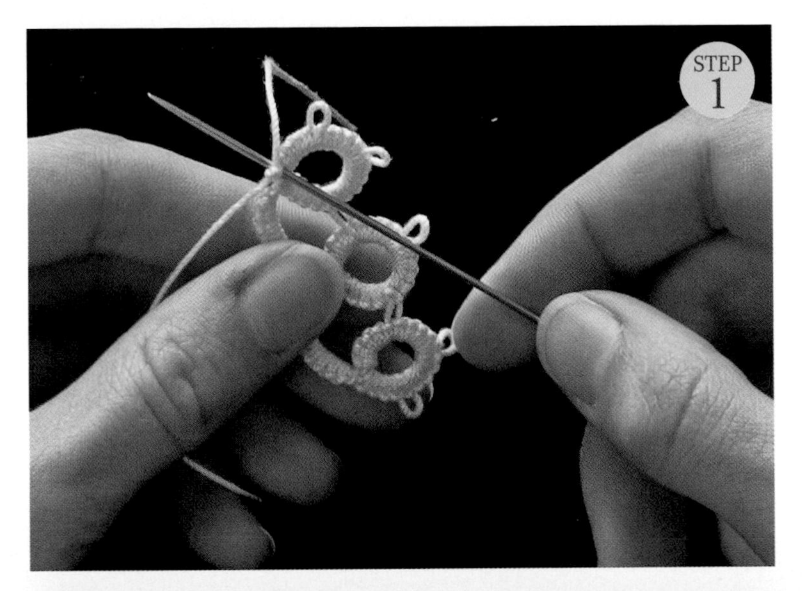

STEP
2

Adding a New Thread or a Different Color

You can only add a new thread after a ring or a chain. For the best transition, add a new thread after a ring.

1. Just cut the needle and ball threads and tie them in a knot. Take your new ball of thread and thread your needle. Push your needle up under the last knot that you made.

2. With a length of thread a couple of feet long on the needle side of the thread, tat the next part of your pattern onto the needle and work as usual, reversing your work and tying a knot. To hide the extra ends of the thread, simply thread them onto a needle and feed them back through some of the already completed double stitches.

PERFE
MASON

Tatted Hankie *Baby Bonnet*

Supply List

1 Tatted Hankie (approximately 10" square)
All-purpose sewing thread in a matching color
Ribbon for ties
Ribbon for small bows

Instructions

1. Fold the hankie in half and lay it flat, with the long hemmed side toward you and the folded edge at the top. Fold each outer top corner down toward the center of the open side (the side closest to you). Now your hankie should be in the shape of a big triangle with two smaller triangles inside of it.
2. Grab each corner of your smaller triangles from the center bottom and fold them up so they touch the outside edge and their top edges are at a 90-degree angle to the center line). Using a few small stitches, sew each outside corner down to the bonnet.
3. Fold the top point of the hat down about 3/4" from the top. Next, invert the fold so that the point of this little triangle is underneath the top layer of the hat. Pin it in place. Place another pin at the point where the two smaller triangles touch in the center of the bonnet. You can now sew small bows onto each of these two points to hold them in place. Be sure that you only sew into the top layer of the hankie (the baby's head will fit in between the two layers of the large triangle shape).
4. Attach ties at each lower corner and decorate with small bows if you desire. You can also add a small box pleat at the back bottom center of the bonnet to give it a rounder shape.

Tatted Hankie

Supply List

1 Hankie or finely woven fabric
Thread #80
Needle # 8

Instructions

First, make a crocheted edging on your hankie or piece of fabric (like the green edging on the hankie at left) by using steps 1 and 2 from our Plate Savers on page 35.

Edging:

R. 3ds, 1p, 3ds, attach to crocheted edging or directly to a hankie, 3ds, 1p, 3ds, Cl, Rw.
*Leave 1/8" thread space between the last ring and where you start the next.
R. 6ds, Cl, Rw.
Leave 1/8" thread.
R. 3ds, j (to picot on left side of ring that is already attached), 3 ds, attach, 3ds, 1p, 3ds, Cl, Rw.*
Repeat from *to*, until only one ring remains to be completed.
R. 6ds, Cl, Rw.
Leave 1/8" of thread. Place a knot at the end, then tie to top of very first ring. Knot and hide ends.

For Shuttle Users:

If you use a shuttle, in place of attaching the tatting directly to the hankie, you can make a picot when the pattern calls for joins or attachments. When you've completed the project, you can then hand stitch the tatting to the handkerchief. The result will be practically the same as with the needle.

Attaching Chains o Buttons:

nsert tatting needle into front of button. Bring thread up from the back and around the top. Reinsert needle through the front of the button in the same hole. Bring needle back up and make a small knot at the top. Start your tatting right at knot.

Attaching Rings o Buttons:

Set button against tatting needle; hold in place using your left hand. Take a small crochet hook and pass t through one buttonhole. Hook the main tatting thread on the back side of the button, and then pull it up through the buttonhole. You should now have a small loop of thread on your crochet hook. Pass the tatting needle through this loop. Remove crochet hook. Tighten tension and slide thread against tatting.

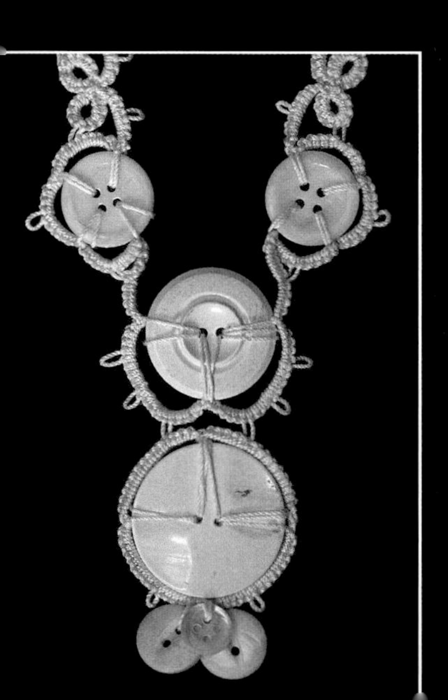

Tatted Button Necklace

Once you've mastered basic tatting, you're ready for the more advanced tatting found in this project.

Supply List

Thread no. 10
Needle no. 5
Very small crochet hook
Buttons: Two 3/4" four-hole, one 1" two-hole, one 1 1/4" two-hole, two 1/2" two-hole, one 3/8" four-hole, one 3/8" shank two hole

Instructions

First Row of Medallion:

Attach (to one 3/4" button using chain attachment directions, left).
Ch. 5ds, 1p, 5ds, attach (to next buttonhole on right).
Ch. 5ds, 1p, 5ds, attach (to next buttonhole on right).
Ch. 5ds, 1p, 5ds, attach (to next buttonhole on right).
Ch. 5ds, j (to picot of previous chain), 5ds, attach (to any hole in the 1" button).
Ch. 5ds, 1p, 5ds, attach (to same buttonhole as previous), attach (to next free buttonhole).
Ch. 5ds, 1p, 5ds, 1p, 5ds, 1p, 5ds, attach (to last previously attached hole).
Ch. 5ds, 1p, 5ds.
Ch. 5ds, j (to free picot of previous chain), attach (to any hole in second 3/4" button).
Ch. 5ds, 1p, 5ds, attach (to next buttonhole on right).
Ch. 5ds, 1p, 5ds, attach (to next hole on right), double knot and hide ends.

Second Row of Medallion:

Attach (to 1 1/4" button, any hole).
Ch. 10ds, 1p, 5ds, attach (to 1/2" button, use directions for attaching rings to buttons, left), 1ds, attach (to four-hole 3/8" button), 1ds, attach (to 1/2" button, using same directions as previous), 5ds, 1p, 10ds, attach (to free hole in large 1 1/4" button, using chain attachment directions).
Ch. 10ds, j (to fifth from the last exposed picot on medallion's first row), 5ds, attach (to 1 1/4" button, in same hole as previous attachment), attach (to next buttonhole).
Ch. 5ds, j (to first picot to the right of previous joining to first row), 10ds.
Tie to start of first chain of second row. Double knot and hide ends.

Necklace Band, Right Side:

R. 5ds, 1p, 5ds, Cl, Rw.
Ch. 5ds, 1p, 5ds, Rw.
*R. 5ds, j (to previous picot), 5ds, Cl.
R. 5ds, 1p, 5ds, Cl, Rw.
Ch. 5ds, 1p, 5ds, Cl, Rw.
R. 5ds, j (to previous picot), 5ds, Cl.*
Repeat from * to * until you have a total of 14 chains and 28 rings.
R. 5ds, j (to very first exposed picot on the top right side of the medallion), 5ds, Cl, Rw.
Ch. 5ds, 1p, 5ds. Tie to base of original chain on the medallion. Double knot and hide ends.

Necklace Band, Left Side:

R. 2ds, attach (to two-hole 3/8" shank button, using ring attachment directions, left), 3ds, 1p, 5ds, Cl, Rw.
Ch. 5ds, 1p, 5ds, Cl, Rw.
*R. 5ds, j (to previous picot), 5ds, Cl.
R. 5ds, 1p, 5ds, Cl, Rw.
Ch. 5ds, 1p, 5ds, Cl, Rw.
R. 5ds, j (to previous picot), 5ds, Cl.*
Repeat from * to * until you have a total of 14 chains and 28 rings.
Rw.
R. 5ds, j (to very first exposed picot on the top left side of the medallion), 5ds, Cl, Rw.
Ch. 5ds, 1p, 5ds. Tie to base of original chain on the medallion. Double knot and hide ends.

Cutwork

Cutwork is a beautiful form of embroidery that involves cutting away the inside of a design that has been outlined with buttonhole stitches. It creates a delicate, romantic, lacy fabric. The simplest form of cutwork is eyelet lace, a pattern of small round holes with a raised outline. You can use the cutwork technique on nearly any type of fabric, although it was traditionally done on cotton flour-sack fabric.

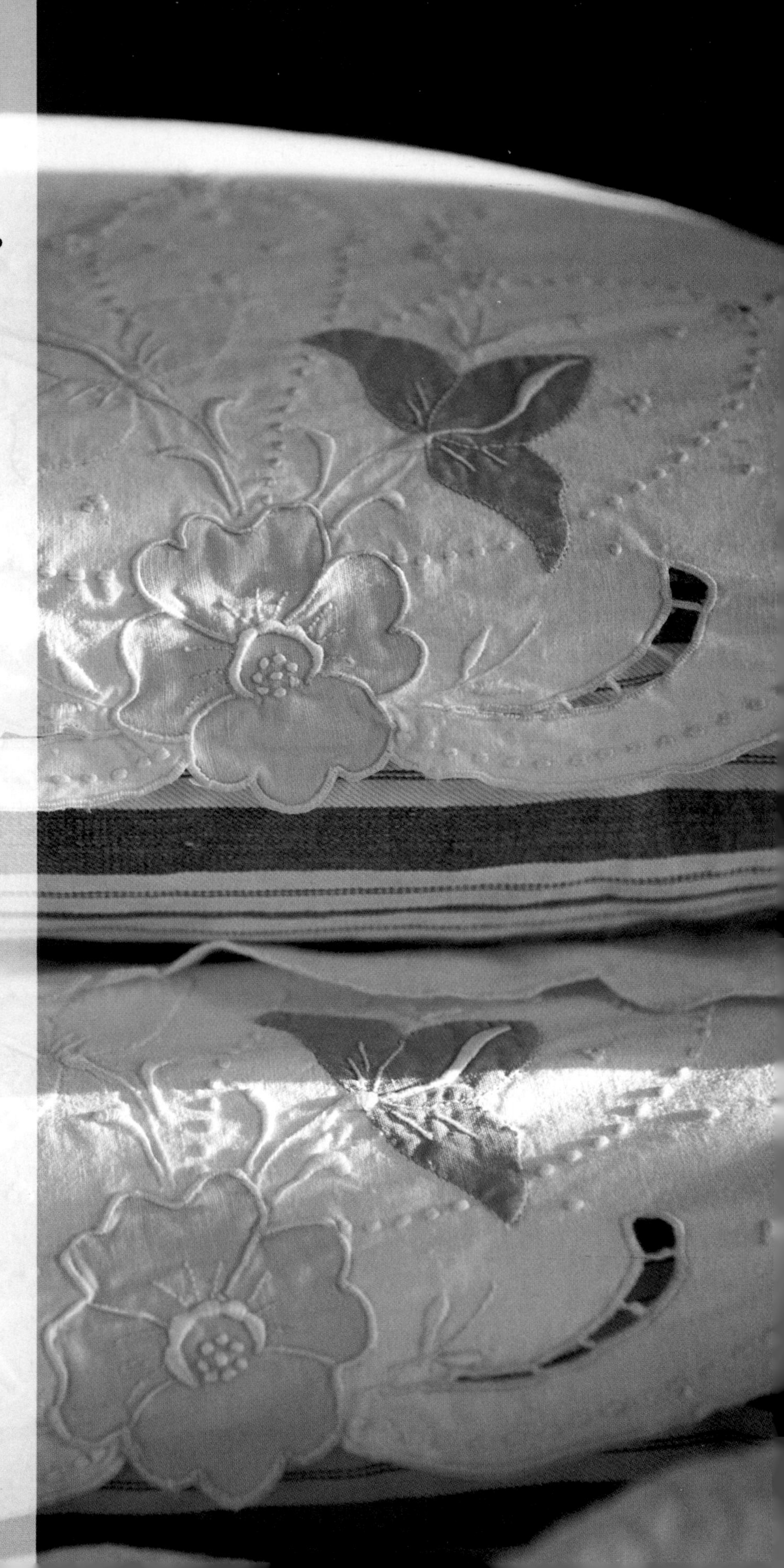

Christening Gown

Erika Frances is an Idaho farmgirl who claims she knows most of the fishing and hiking spots our state has to offer. Married to a wheat farmer for seventeen years, Erika is striking out on her own. Now that her youngest of four children is a teenager, Erika is enrolled in the graduate student program at Washington State University, majoring in apparel and design. Currently she has a blossoming home business selling handmade christening gowns, baby bonnets, and dresses. Erika uses repurposed antique pillowcases made from natural cottons, linens, or silks for the body of her gowns. She then sews each bodice to match the stitches she finds in the pillowcases, using techniques like cutwork, smocking, drawnwork, and pin tucks. "All the old stitches," she says. On the following page, she shares her gown pattern, but encourages you to look her up if you haven't the time to make one yourself. And if you have some vintage pillowcases that need a new home, drop her a line at erikafiiams@hotmail.com.

CHRISTENING *Gown*

Christening gowns are also known across rural America as "pillowcase dresses." To convert our pattern into a pillowcase dress for an older child, simply shorten the length and increase the bodice and sleeve size.

Supply List

1 pillowcase (king size makes a nice long gown)
2 yards ribbon
1 yard small bias tape in matching or contrasting color, optional

Assembling, Stitching, and Finishing Details

(1/2" seam allowance unless otherwise indicated)

1. Lay your pattern pieces on your pillowcase close to the closed end. Remember to take into account how many of each piece you need (noted on pattern pieces) and that you have a double layer of fabric. Also, if you wish to work any type of embellishment on the Bodice Front piece, you will have to make sure there are about 4" to spare widthwise. Set your pattern pieces aside for the moment. Cut off the top of your pillowcase. Undo the side seams and the top seam. Cut out a rectangle of fabric that is as tall as the Bodice Front piece and about 4" wider. Set aside. Cut the rest of your pattern pieces from the remaining fabric.
2. Fold sleeves on the lines indicated on the pattern piece toward the center of the sleeve (direction indicated by the arrows) to form center pleat, and press. Baste top and bottom of the sleeve to hold the pleat in place. Turn under the long straight edge of both sleeves 1/4" twice and stitch (this is the edge of the sleeve). Alternatively, you could trim off the 1/2" seam allowance and finish this edge with bias tape, piping, or lace. Fold each sleeve in half with right sides of the fabric together, matching up the short edges. Stitch along the short edges. This is the seam along the underside of the sleeve. (You could also finish with a French seam.)
3. Embellish the piece of fabric you've set aside for the bodice front with vertical rows of cutwork, pin tucks, and decorative stitches. For a pin tuck, simply press your fabric in a fold vertically and stitch very close to the folded edge. You can thread ribbon through rows of cutwork as in our example if you wish. After you've embellished to your heart's content, lay your Bodice Front pattern piece on the fabric, taking care to make sure that the embellishing is perfectly vertical. Cut out the Bodice Front piece.
4. On both Bodice Back pieces, turn under the center back edges 1/4" twice and press, making sure you create a left and a right side. Stitch.
5. With the right sides of the fabric together, pin the Bodice Back pieces to the Bodice Front. The shoulders and sides should match up, and the center backs of the Bodice Back pieces should touch but not overlap. Stitch the shoulders and the sides.
6. To finish the neck opening, cut a strip of bias tape long enough to go around it plus 1". Match up the raw edges of the bias tape and the raw edges of the neck opening at one side of the Bodice Back (insert piping or lace between the bodice and tape, also with raw edges matching, for a more decorative finish) and sew a 1/4" seam around the entire neck opening until you are close to the other back edge. When you know

where the end will be, stop and cut the bias tape so the end will match up with the back edge plus 1/4"; tuck the 1/4" into the middle of the bias tape, and continue sewing to the end. Press the bias tape to the inside of the bodice and topstitch. Tack bottom edge if desired.

7. Before joining sleeves to bodice, it might help to baste tops of sleeves first to ease in any fullness, leaving thread ends long enough to gather slightly.

8. With the bodice fabric wrong side out and the sleeves right side out, stick one sleeve into one sleeve hole. Match up the center of the pleat on the sleeve with the shoulder seam on the bodice, and match up the lower seam on the sleeve with the side seam on the bodice, easing in fullness; pin. Stitch. Repeat with the other sleeve.

9. Now you have to attach the skirt part of the pillowcase to the bodice. Start by turning the bodice and the pillowcase wrong side out. Fold the bodice in half down the middle, and the pillowcase in half lengthwise. Now, match up the bottom edge of the bodice with the top raw edge of the pillowcase. Making sure to take into account the 1/2" seam allowance and allowing for fullness, cut the pillowcase to the correct size to sew onto the bottom of the bodice. Angle your cut down to the lower corners of the pillowcase (at the open end). Stitch the front and the back of the pillowcase together. Keep the skirt part wrong side out and turn the bodice right side out. Put the bodice inside the skirt (the right side of the bodice should be facing the right side of the skirt) and match up the raw edges. If one side of your pillowcase is embellished, make sure that it is matched up with the front of the bodice. Make adjustments as necessary if your skirt doesn't fit perfectly with the bodice, gathering the top of the skirt to the fullness desired. Pin in place and stitch. Press the seam toward the bottom of the gown.

10. Turn the gown right side out. Pin ribbon onto the gown to cover up the seam between the bodice and the skirt. Topstitch in place near each edge of the ribbon.

11. Cut the remaining ribbon in half. Sew one piece near the top of the center back opening on one side, and the other piece opposite it on the other side. This is to tie the center back closed.

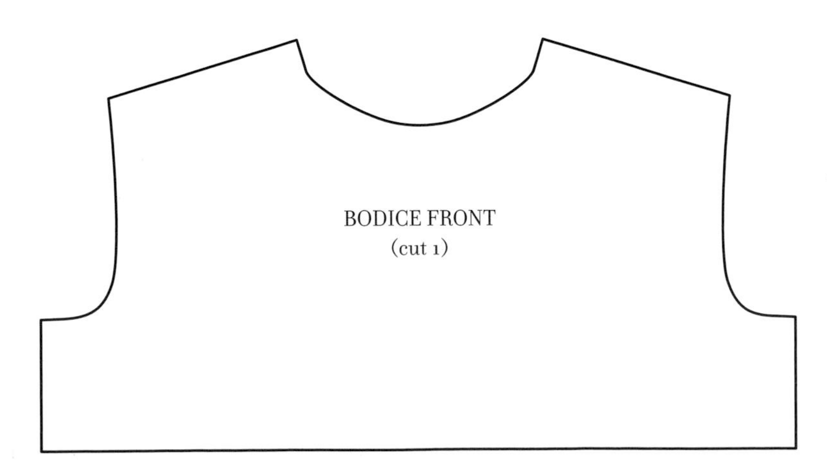

Make a copy of this page; then enlarge it 300 percent for your life-size MaryJanesFarm pattern.

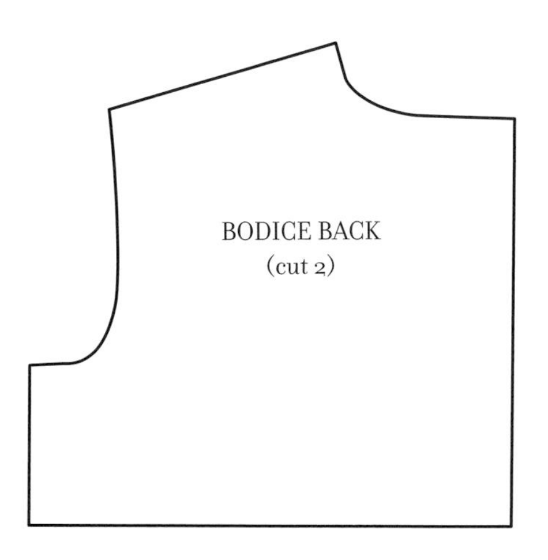

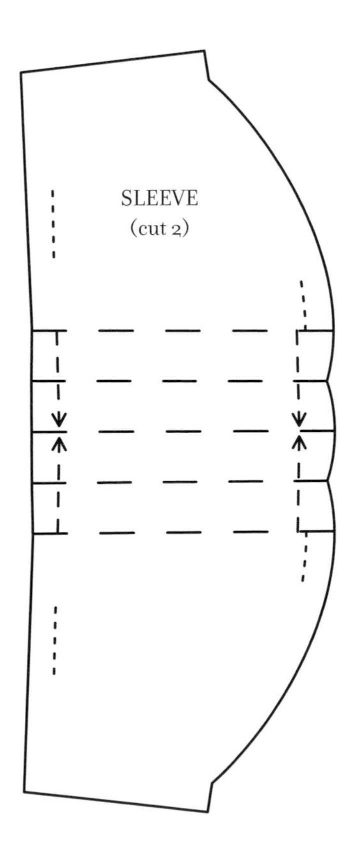

WEARABLE *Cutwork*

Instructions

1. Trace the design below onto the garment of your choice.
2. Create the flower petals using a filler stitch (page 54).
3. Create the stems using an outline stitch (page 54).
4. To create the smaller flowers and the center of the larger flower, outline them with a basting stitch.
5. Cover the basting stitches with buttonhole stitches (page 54) that are worked very close together. These stitches are what will keep your fabric from fraying apart when you cut the middles out, so keeping the stitches close together will help.
3. After you've outlined everything with buttonhole stitches, cut out the middles (the black areas in the pattern) with a very sharp pair of small scissors. It might help to start your cut with a seam ripper or a small razor blade.

Note: For a tatted edge, as on the bolero at left, see page 109.

If any of our yesteryear handiwork projects have your name written all over them, but you're feeling as if you want to start small, make a holiday ornament. For example, crochet the size hexagon listed for the scarf, starch it, then hang your "snowflake" on a friend's holiday tree. Or decorate an entire tree in yo-yos! Make yo-yos (leave them plain or embellish with beads and buttons), starch, and hang. Or for Easter, make a papier-mâché egg; glue a tiny double-sided ruffle on it, end to end; and edge the ruffle in tatting.

Crochet *Basics*

Traveling? Once you've begun a project using my step-by-step detailed crochet instructions, you can hit the road using a printable, condensed version available for free on my website at www.maryjanesfarm.org/StitchingRoom.

Crochet threads and yarns are all over the map and can be confusing. Worsted, 2-ply, No. 30—what's a crocheter to do? Here's our translation:

Crochet **threads** are identified by numbers: 3, 5, 8, 10, 20, 30, 40, and up; the lower the number, the thicker the thread. Early crochet was used for delicate projects like doilies, so crochet threads were thin and were used with the smaller steel crochet hooks.

Modern-day crochet involves thicker thread (yarn) and big, chunky hooks used for sweaters, afghans, and more. **Yarns** come in fine, medium, and heavy weights. Fine yarn is often referred to as baby, fingering, or 2-ply. Sport or 3-ply yarns are medium-fine weight. Worsted or 4-ply yarns are medium weight. Bulky and chunky are heavy yarns meant for the largest needles. There are also many new variable-textured yarns that defy any of these categories. Like the modern-day cold-cereal aisle in a grocery store, the choices are plentiful!

How to Read a Crochet Pattern

Crochet patterns are usually written using the abbreviations on the facing page so the wording doesn't take up too much space. At first, patterns might look like some kind of strange code, but they're quite easy to read once you familiarize yourself with the abbreviations.

A simple pattern for a scarf might start out like this:

Supply List

2 skeins Patons Divine (bulky) yarn, Icicle White, or similar style yarn of your choice

Size J/10 (6 mm) crochet hook or size needed to obtain gauge

Blunt-tip needle for weaving in ends

Gauge: 4" x 4" = 11 stitches and 6 rows worked in double crochet

Instructions

Ch 19.

Row 1: Dc in fourth ch from hook, dc in each ch after. Turn.

Row 2: Ch 3, dc in each st. Turn.

Here's what it means:
The **Supply List** simply lists what you'll need for the project. It will tell you what kind of yarn to use and how much of it to buy. It also lists the correct size of hook and any other supplies you may need. Larger hooks—usually made of colored aluminum, bone, wood, or plastic—have sizes indicated by both letters and numbers; the higher the number and letter, the larger the size. Smaller hooks are made of steel and are best for finer threads—16 is the smallest size, and 00 is the largest.

Gauge tells you how big or small the pattern creator's stitches were when they made the pattern. (Some people crochet in tight, tiny stitches; others crochet in grand, loose loops.) Testing your style for gauge is very important when you're making a sweater, socks, mittens, or anything else that has to be an exact size to fit right. It's not as important for things like scarves and dishrags. The gauge tells you how many stitches and rows make up a 4" square in a particular stitch with a particular size of hook. It's always a good idea to make a gauge test swatch before you start a project so your adult-size sweater will fit you and not a small child, or vice versa. To do this, simply make a foundation chain that is a few stitches longer than the number of stitches in the gauge swatch and work the piece in the required stitches until it is longer than 4". Then, measure how many stitches and rows are in a 4" square. If you have more stitches than the gauge calls for, your stitches are too small and you should retest your gauge with a hook that is one size larger. If you have too few stitches or rows, go down a hook size and try again. Trust me, testing your gauge will save a lot of heartache in the long run—there is nothing worse than finishing a beautiful sweater, only to end up with sleeves that are too short or long once you put it on.

The **Instructions** section is the actual pattern. "Ch 19" means you should work 19 chain stitches for your foundation chain. For Row 1, "Dc in fourth ch from hook" means to make your first double crochet stitch into the fourth chain from the hook, and "dc in each ch after" means to make one double crochet into each of the remaining chain stitches. "Turn" is simple: just turn your work around horizontally. For Row 2, "Ch 3, dc in each st. Turn." means you are to chain three stitches for your turning chain, make a double crochet in each stitch to the end of the row, and turn.

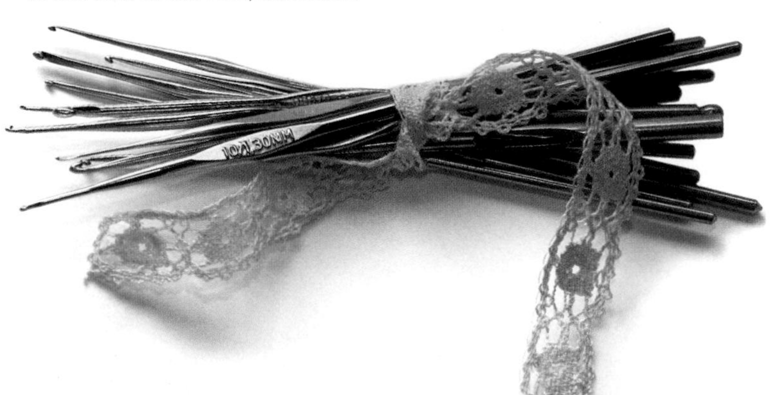

Crochet Guidelines

Basics:

1. Our instructions are written for right-handed stitchers. If you're left-handed, simply reverse your hook and yarn positions.
2. When making your foundation chain, do not count the loop on the hook.
3. Always insert your hook into a stitch from front to back.
4. Always insert your hook under the two top loops of a stitch, unless noted otherwise (see diagram on page 58).
5. At the end of a row of stitches, always turn your work from right to left to begin the next row.

Abbreviations:

beg – beginning (of a round, row, or pattern)
CC – contrasting color, second less prominent yarn in a pattern
ch, chs – chain stitch or chains
dc – double crochet
dec – decrease
hdc – half double crochet
inc – increase
MC – main color, most prominent yarn in a pattern
rep – repeat
rnd, rnds – round or rounds
sc – single crochet
sk – skip
sl st – slip stitch
sp, sps – space, spaces (referring to making a stitch in a chain space or the space between two stitches instead of directly into a stitch)
st, sts – stitch, stitches
tch – turning chain
tog – together
tr – triple crochet
yo – yarn over
* * instructions between asterisks are repeated

TWINE BY DAY

Fine by Night

"One woman who lives on a little farm in Lake County, Illinois, does all the work of her farm. Dressed in a skirt that reaches the top of a pair of high-laced coarse shoes, and with her head in a sunbonnet, she plowed the land for five acres of oats, five of corn, and a ten-acre fruit and vegetable patch. She did all her own cultivating, cut fifteen acres of Timothy grass with a mowing machine, raked it, loaded it, and hauled it to her barn. She cares for and milks eleven head of cow, and takes care of a variety of poultry. She lives alone and attends to all her own housework. Rising at five, she works all day, rain or shine, reads her papers after supper, and retires at nine. Now she is 55-years-old and doesn't look a day over two score. She is probably the happiest woman in Lake County. It has been the work of these such nervy and muscular women that rich crops this year have saved."

– "Farm and Fireside," October 1906

Position Your Hands in either of the positions below.

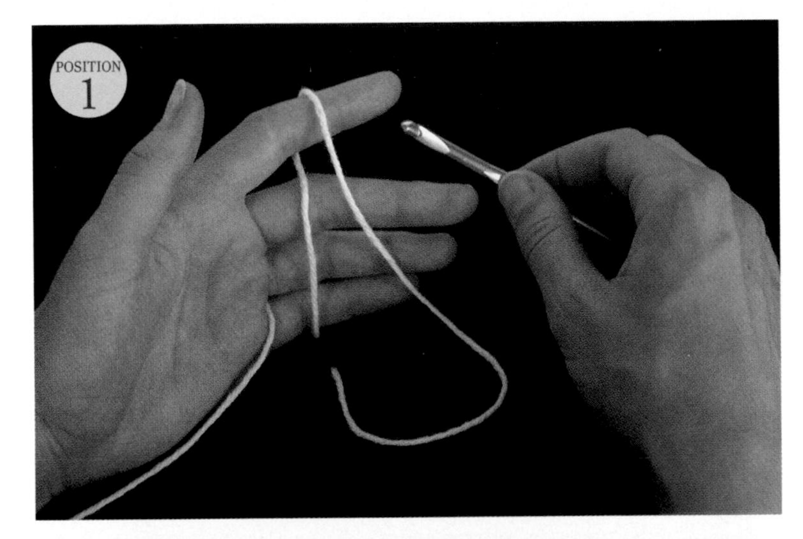

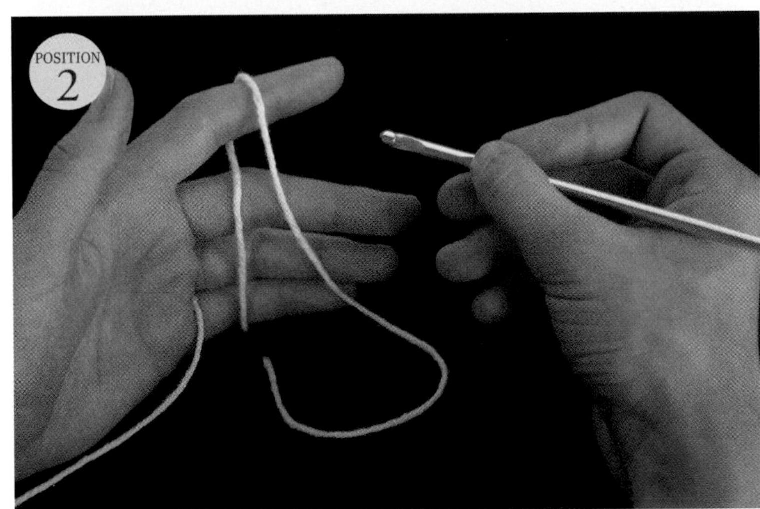

Start with a Slip Knot (right)

1. Hold the ball end of the yarn in your left hand with the tail end of the yarn hanging off to the right. Make a loop by crossing the tail end over the ball end.
2. Let the tail end fall behind the loop so the yarn is bent into a pretzel shape. Hold the crochet hook in your right hand. Stick the hook into the loop and catch the tail end of the yarn with the end of the hook.
3. Holding both ends of the yarn in your left hand, pull the hook (with the yarn still on it) through the loop.
4. Continue pulling until the loop tightens into a knot. You can adjust the size of the knot by pulling on the tail end. You will want this knot to be about the same size as your chain stitches, since it will be the first stitch of your foundation chain. Experiment by making a slip knot and a few chain stitches to find the optimum size for your project.

Make a Slip Knot

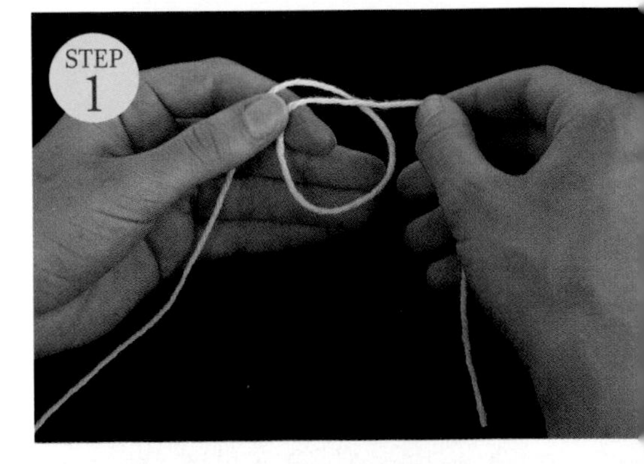

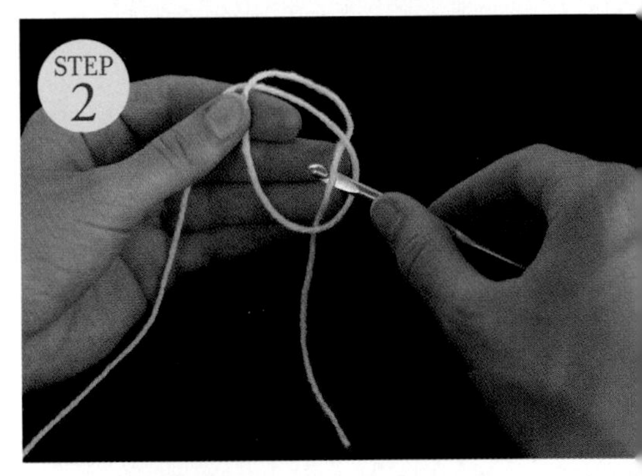

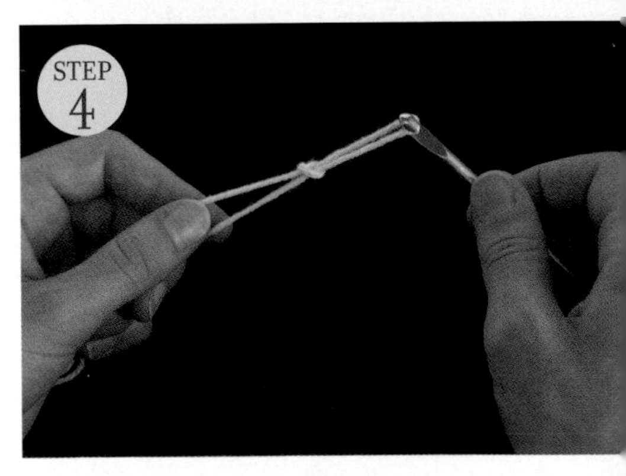

Building Your Foundation Chain (ch)

When you crochet, you will be making a pattern of interlocking loops. To work these loops, the hook is held in one hand, and the yarn is held in the other. The hand that holds the yarn provides tension and supports the work where the hook enters it.

1. After you make a slip knot, the next step is to build a foundation chain, which will become the first row of your crochet. The chain stitches should be uniform and formed loosely enough that the hook can enter each stitch easily when you crochet your second row. Position your hands as shown previously and pinch the tail end of the yarn between your thumb and middle finger directly below the slip knot.

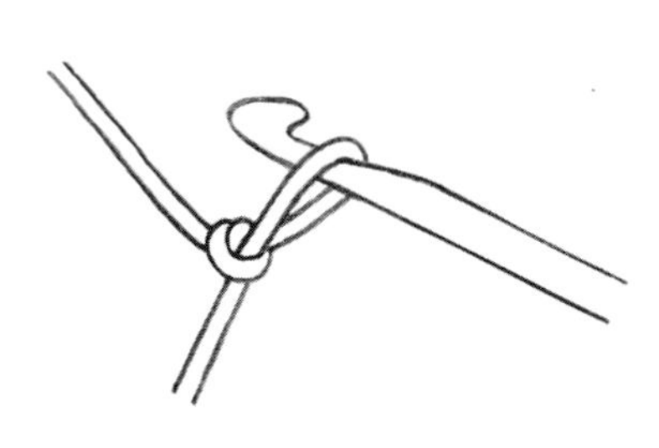

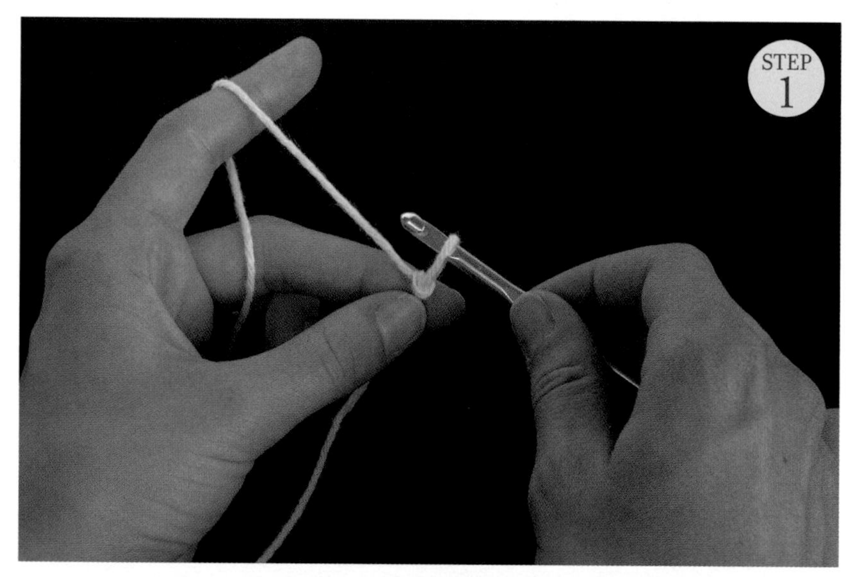

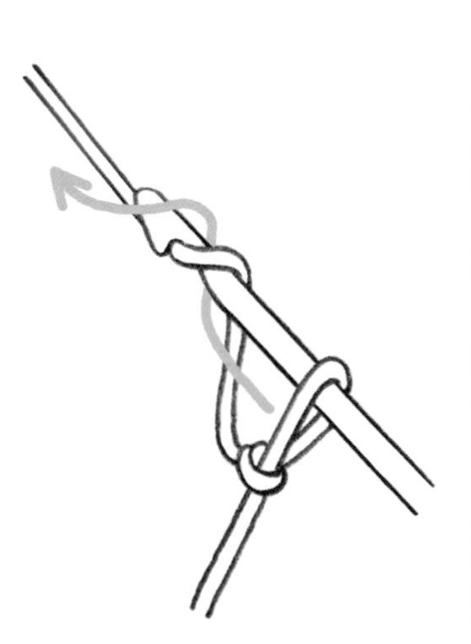

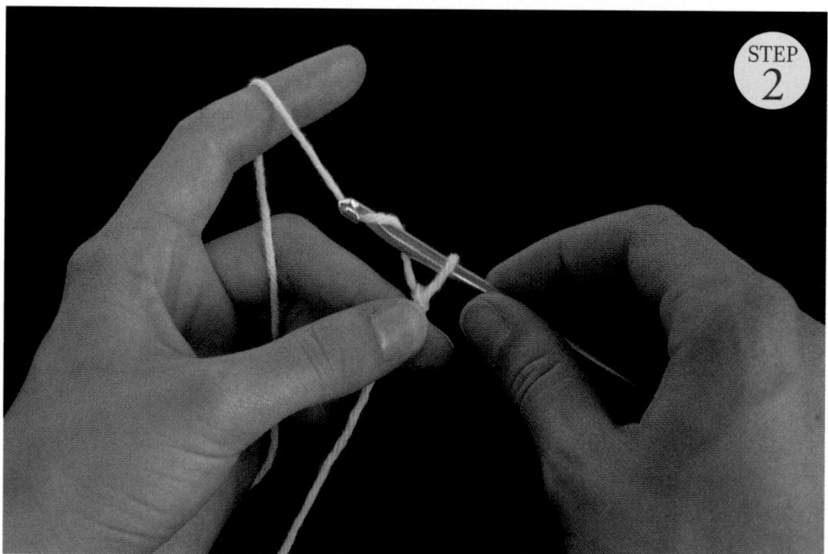

2. To start the chain, pass the hook in front of the yarn leading from the knot up to your index finger. Then pass the hook behind the yarn and pull the hook slightly toward you, catching the yarn under the lip of the hook. This method of using the hook to wrap the yarn around it is called a "yarn over" (yo) and is an integral part of crochet.
3. Keeping the ball yarn taut, draw the hook (and the yarn) through the slip-knot loop, creating a new loop on the hook. The new loop should be loose enough so that the next chain stitch can draw through it easily.
4. Repeat this process, moving your thumb and finger up the chain to hold it as you go, until the chain is as long as your pattern requires (the loop on the hook does not count as part of the total). Practice until you are able to crochet a foundation chain with uniform stitches.

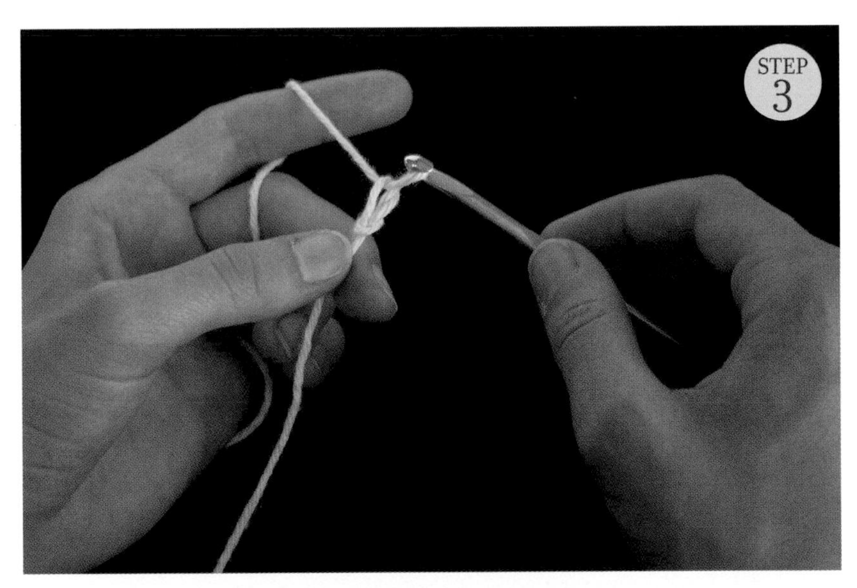

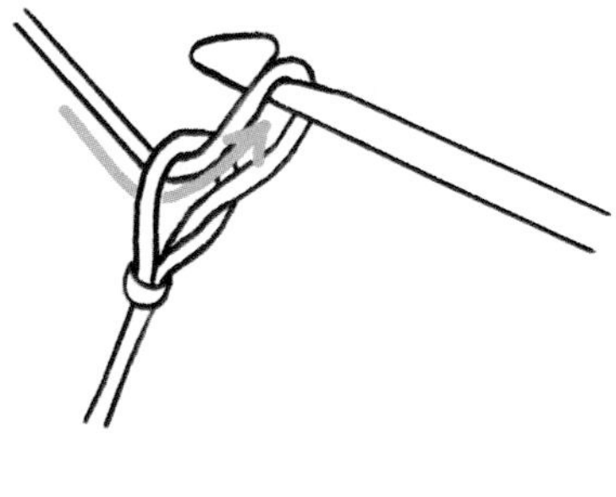

Working into the Foundation Chain

After building your foundation chain, you'll then work into that chain for your next row. The books we've seen are very vague about exactly how to do this. We've provided drawings *and* photos to make this process clearer. Some instructions have you build onto the foundation chain by slipping the crochet hook under *one* loop rather than our *two* loops. (Refer to our photos and drawings below to see what I'm talking about. It's like slipping your hook under a braid.) Slipping your crochet hook under the "braid" (two loops on top, leaving one on the bottom) definitely feels a bit awkward on your first pass, but this method of building "fabric" will give you a stronger, neater, more even look.

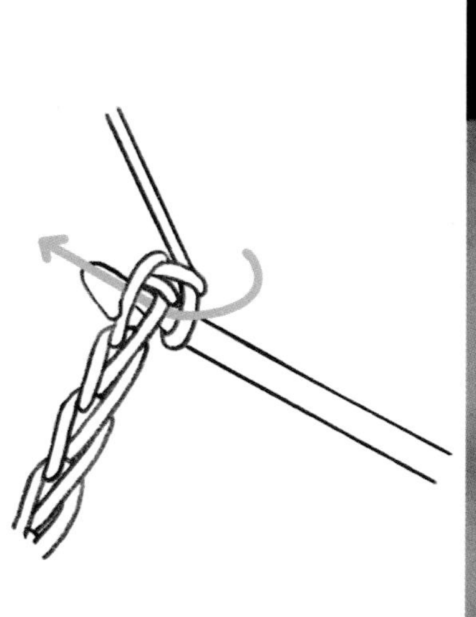

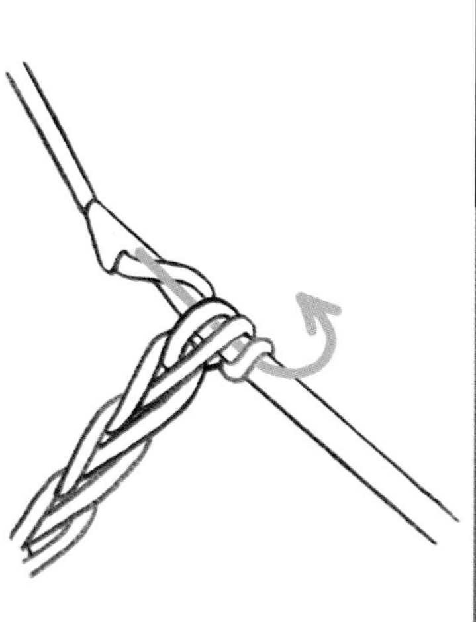

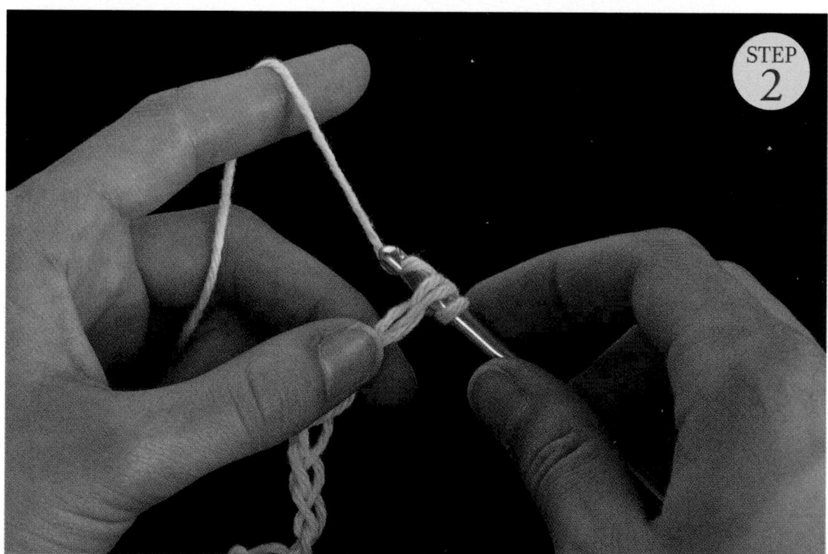

Making a Slip Stitch (sl st)

A slip stitch is the shortest and densest of all the stitches. It is not often used for an entire project; more likely, you will use it to attach pieces together or attach the beginning and the end of a round (page 132).

1. Insert your hook into the second chain from the hook as shown at left.
2. Yarn over.
3. Pull the hook through the chain and the loop on the hook.
4. Repeat by putting the hook through the next chain, yarning over, and pulling the hook through the chain and loop on the hook again. Repeat with every chain stitch until you reach the end of your chain.

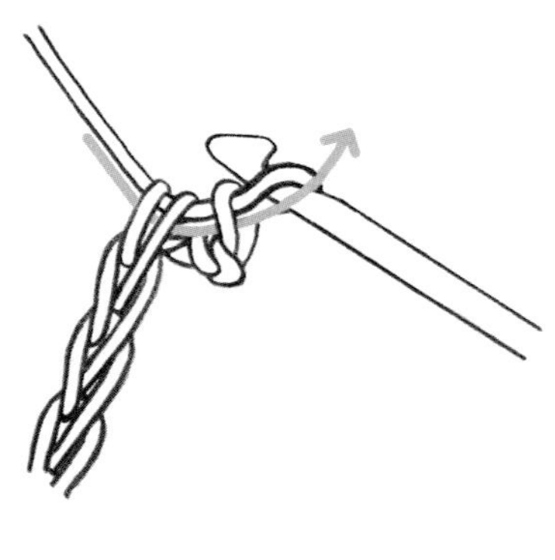

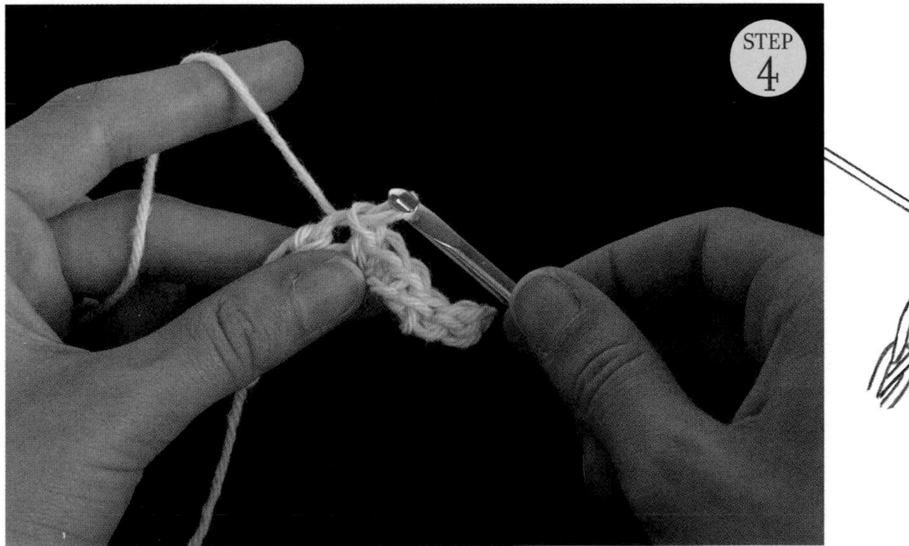

Working a Single Crochet (sc)

A single crochet is still dense but is much more pliable than a slip stitch and makes a firm, flat fabric. It is approximately as wide as it is tall, so it is easy to eyeball how many stitches you'll need for a dishcloth or a similar project.

1. Insert your hook into the second chain from the hook, just like you would for a slip stitch. Yarn over and pull the hook through just the chain. You should have two loops left on your hook.

2. Yarn over again and pull your hook through both of the loops on the hook.

3. You have completed one single crochet!

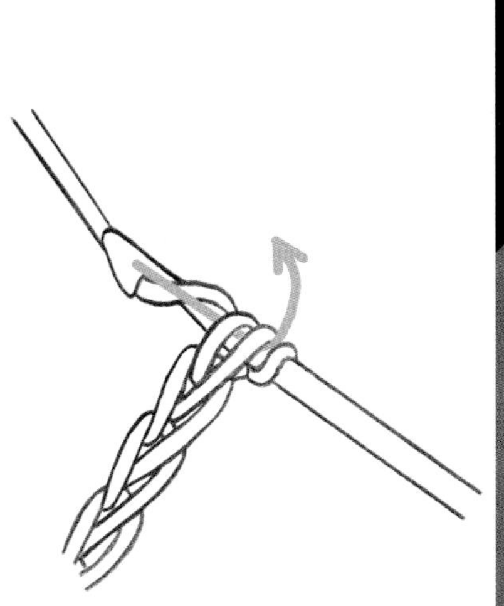

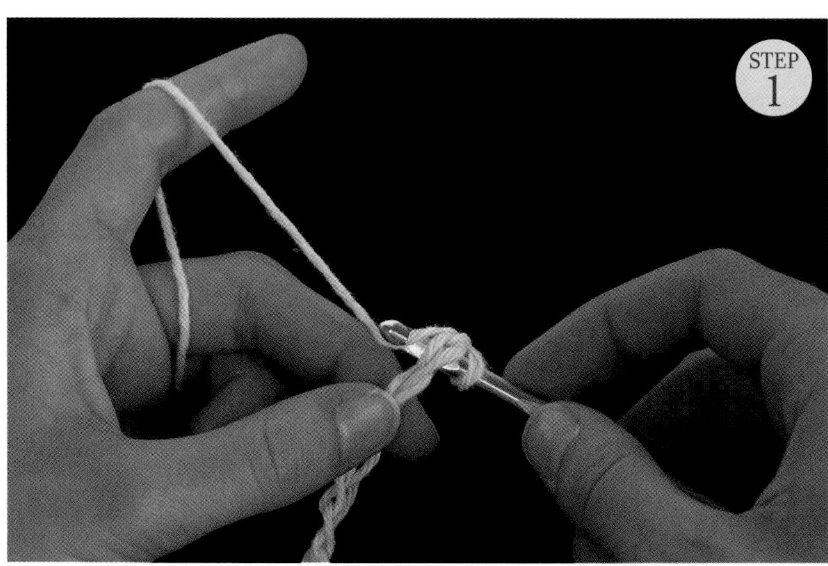

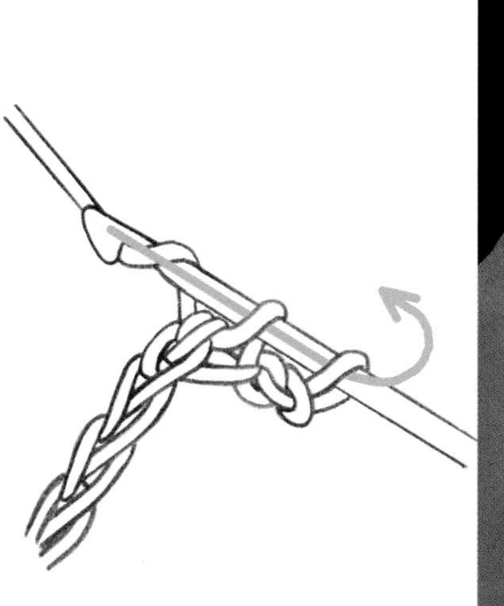

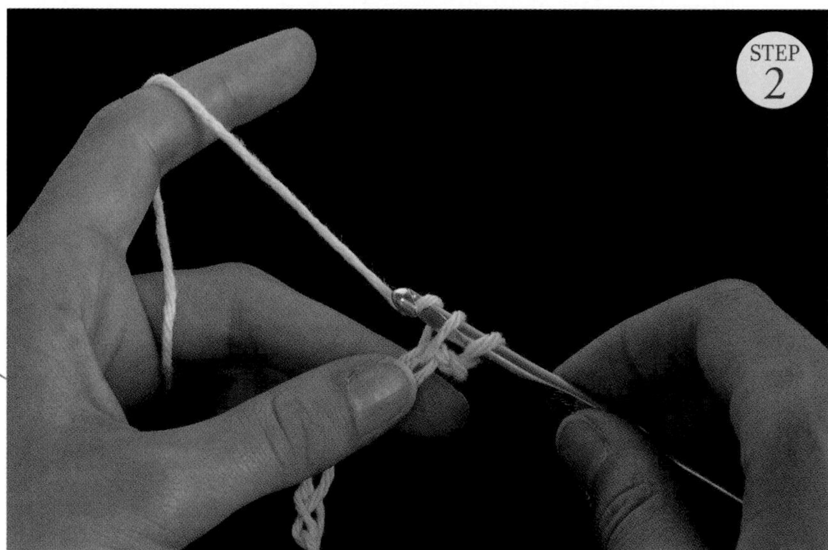

4. To work an entire row, simply make another single crochet, as in steps 1–3, into each chain stitch.

Second Row of Single Crochet

When you get to the end of your first row, simply flip (turn) the work horizontally. You will have to make one chain stitch (just like in a foundation chain) to compensate for the height of a single crochet stitch; otherwise your work will end up all scrunched together on the sides. This is called a "turning chain." Work one single crochet into both top loops ("under the braid" again) of every single crochet from the previous row.

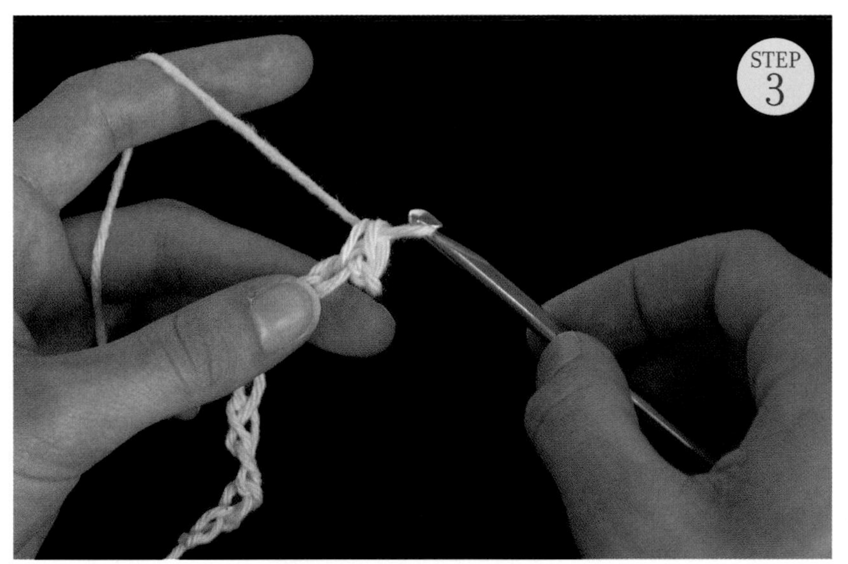

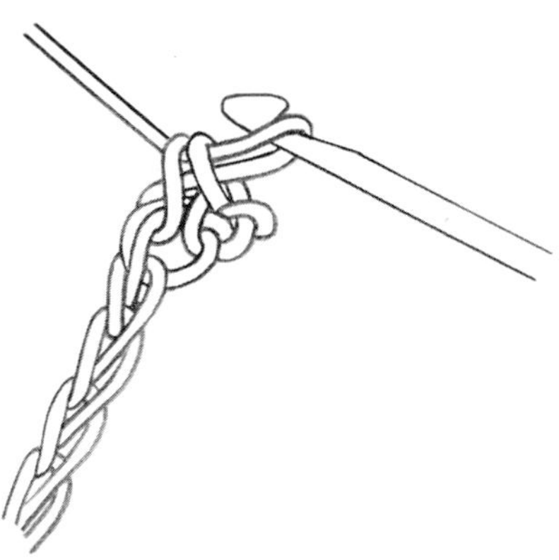

Working a Double Crochet (dc)

A double crochet is taller than a single and creates a much more open, flexible fabric.

1. After making a foundation chain, yarn over and insert the hook into the fourth chain from the hook. (You skip the first three chains just at the beginning of the row to compensate for the height of a double crochet stitch.) There are now three loops on the hook (the two strands of the chain count as one loop): the original loop, the yarn over, and the chain.

2. Yarn over again and pull the hook through the chain. Now there are three loops left on the hook. Yarn over again and pull the hook through two loops.

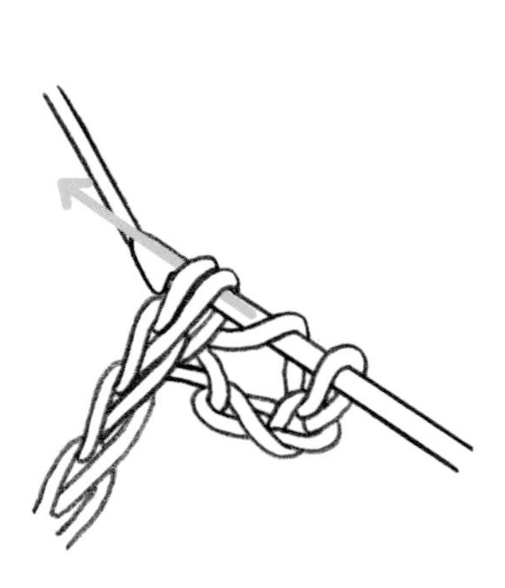

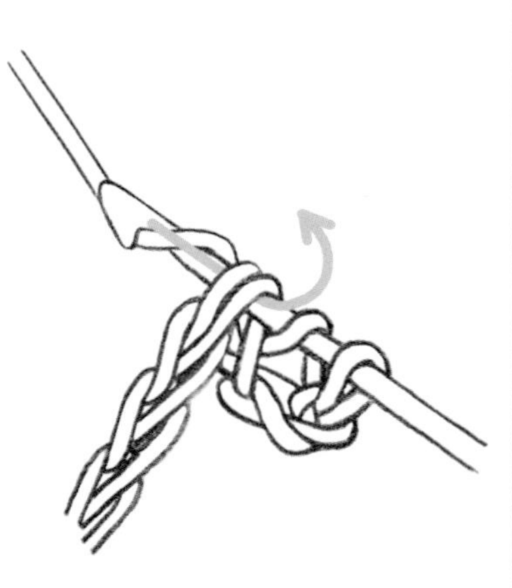

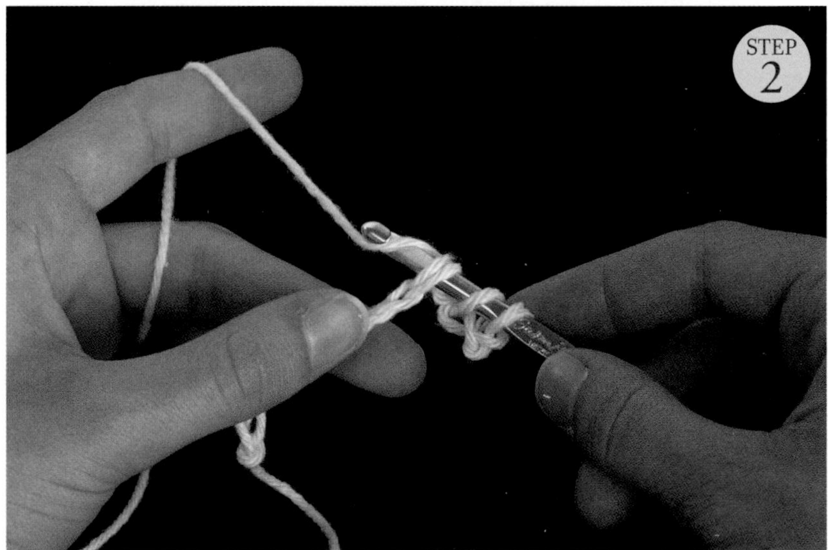

3. Yarn over again and pull the hook through the remaining two loops.
4. You have completed one double crochet!

Work more double crochets into the top of each chain stitch just like you did for the single crochets. When you get to the end of the row, turn the work over to begin the next row. Chain three (your turning chain), skip over the first stitch, and work a double crochet into the top of the next one. Continue working double crochets into the top of each stitch until the end of the row. When you get to the end of the row, work your last stitch into the top of the three-chain piece that you skipped over at the beginning of step 1 (that was a turning chain for the very beginning). Work more rows by following this process.

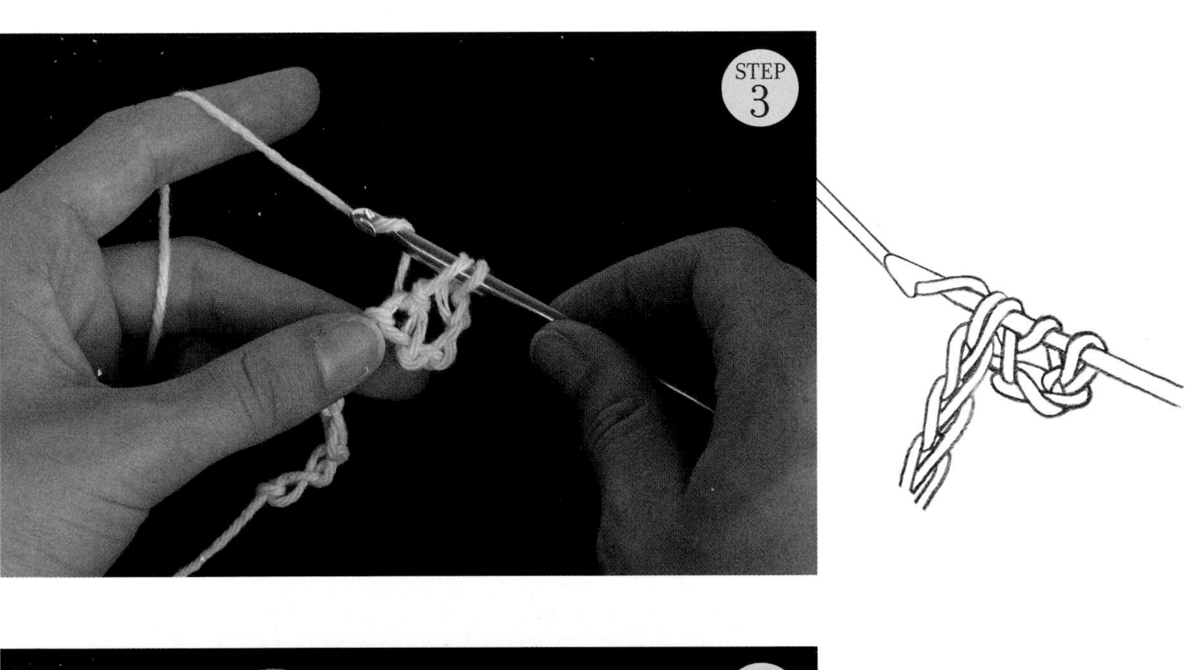

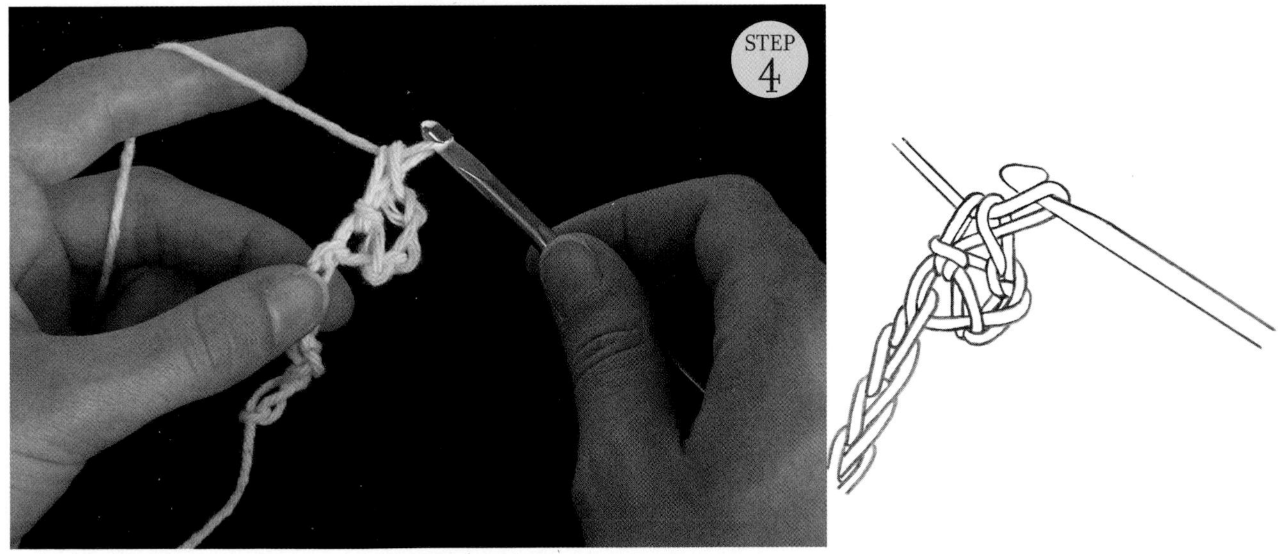

Working a Half Double Crochet (hdc)

This stitch is very similar to a double crochet. It is a little taller than a single crochet, but a little bit shorter than a double, and produces a ridge in its texture. Work just like you would a double crochet, but in step 1, insert the hook into the third chain from the hook instead of the fourth. In step 2, yarn over and pull the hook through all three loops on the hook instead of just two. You should end up with just one loop on the hook if you have done this correctly.

Working a Triple (or Treble) Crochet (tr)

This stitch is a bit taller than a double crochet and produces an airy, open stitch. Work it like a double crochet, but in step 1, yarn over twice and insert the hook into the fifth chain from the hook instead of the fourth. There should be four loops on the hook now instead of just three. Yarn over once and pull through two loops, yarn over again and pull through two more, and yarn over one last time and pull the hook through the last two loops. You have completed one triple crochet!

Increasing (inc)

1. To increase the number of stitches in a row of your work to make it bigger, simply work two stitches into one stitch of the previous row. This can be done at the beginning, end, or in the middle of a row. This example shows it at the end of a row.

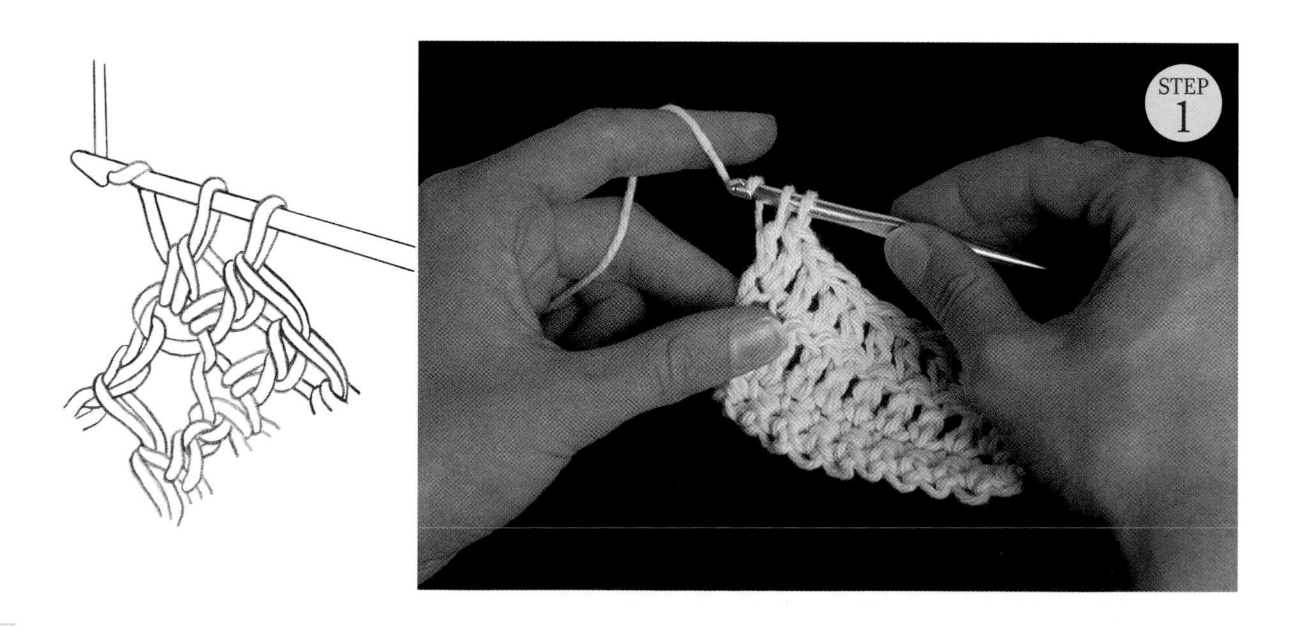

Decreasing (dec)

1. To decrease the number of stitches in a row of your work to make it smaller, just work one stitch into two stitches of the previous row: slide your hook through the tops of two stitches instead of just one at the beginning of your stitch.
2. This can be done at the beginning, end, or middle of a row. This example shows it at the end of a row.

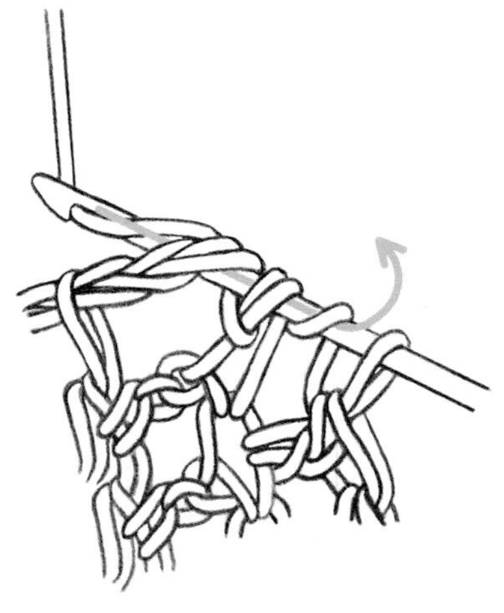

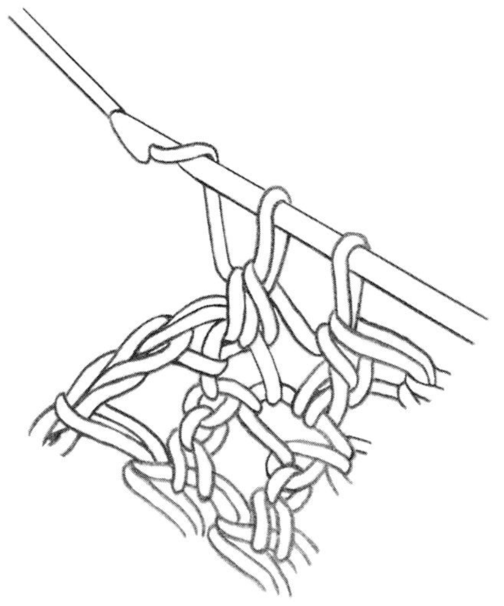

Working in Rounds (rnd)

1. Make a short foundation chain (the pattern will designate how many, usually from four to six). Insert the hook into the first chain you made, but instead of going under the "braid" for this stitch, go directly down into the top of the chain stitch so that your round lays flat.
2. Yarn over and pull through all the loops on the hook.
3. If you are working in single crochet, make one chain for height (two for half double, three for double, four for triple). Work the number of stitches called for in the pattern by inserting your hook right into the middle of the ring and not into the chains that are making up the

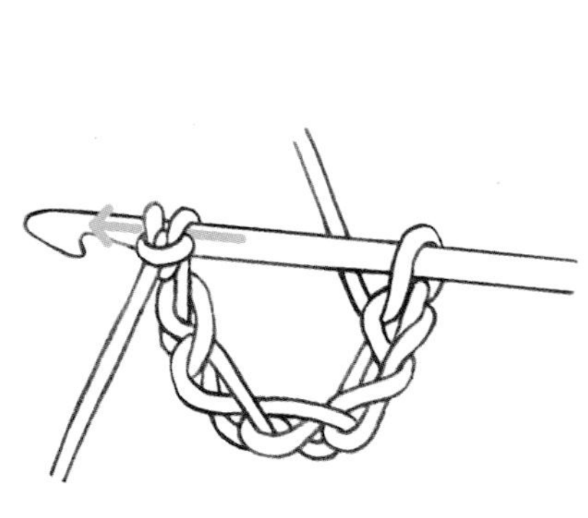

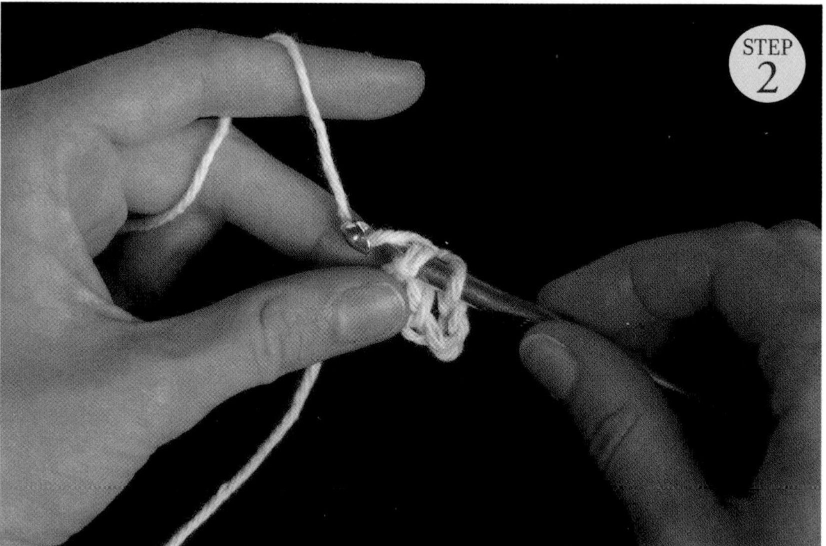

ring. Attach the last stitch of your round to the first stitch with a slip stitch at the top.

4. When working in rounds, it's sometimes hard to tell where one row ends and the next begins. Drape a little scrap of different-colored yarn at the end of a row before you start the next one to mark your place. Make one chain for height and work as many single crochets into the top of each stitch as indicated in the pattern. To keep a circle flat, you will have to make more stitches in each consecutive row than in the previous one (your pattern will specify how many); otherwise, you'll end up with a kind of cylinder-shaped object.

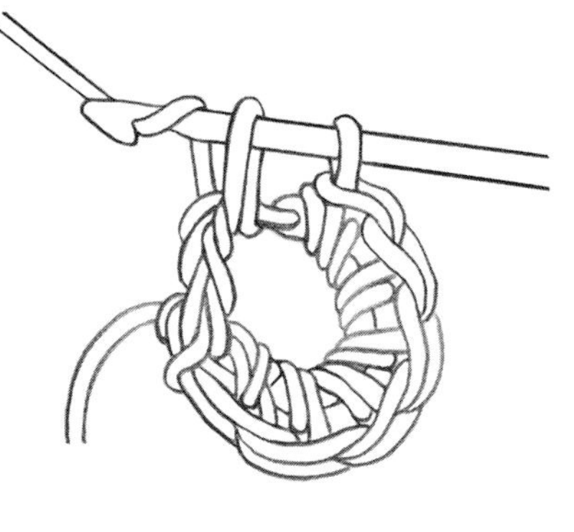

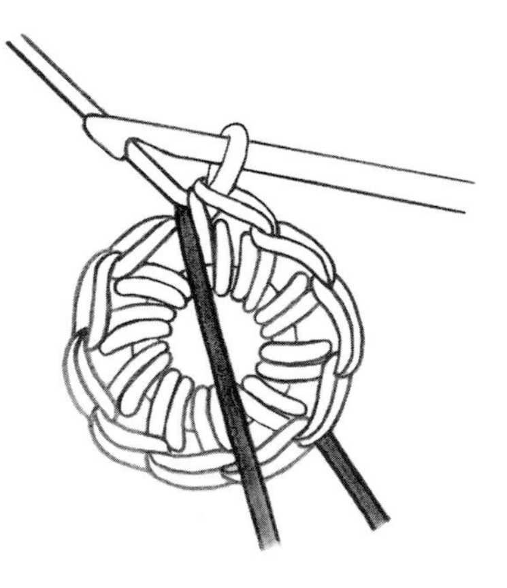

Working in a New Ball of Yarn

You can use this method to change yarn in the middle of a row or at the end of one. These photographs show how to do it in the middle of a row of single crochet.

1. After you complete a stitch but before you start a new one, start holding your new yarn right along with your old one. The tail of the new yarn should stick off to the right.
2. Pretend that the old and new yarns are one and the same. Yarn over with both yarns and insert your hook into the top of the next stitch.
3. Drop the old yarn and yarn over with just the new one. Pull through both loops on the hook.

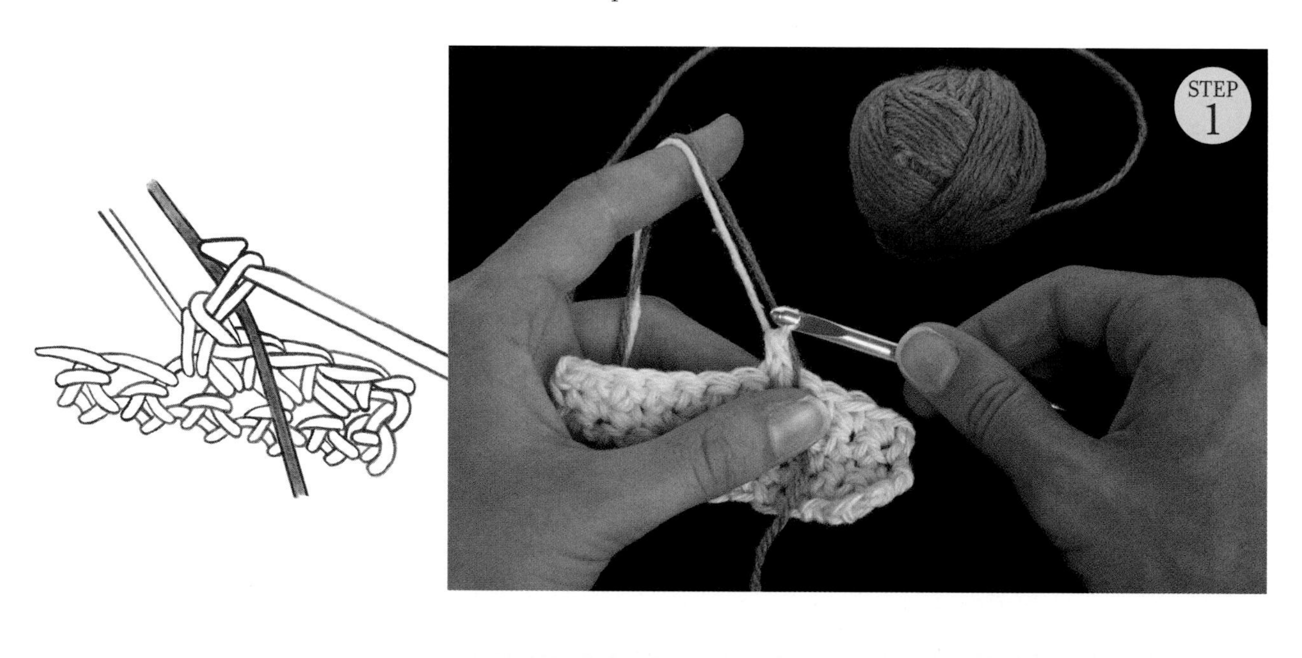

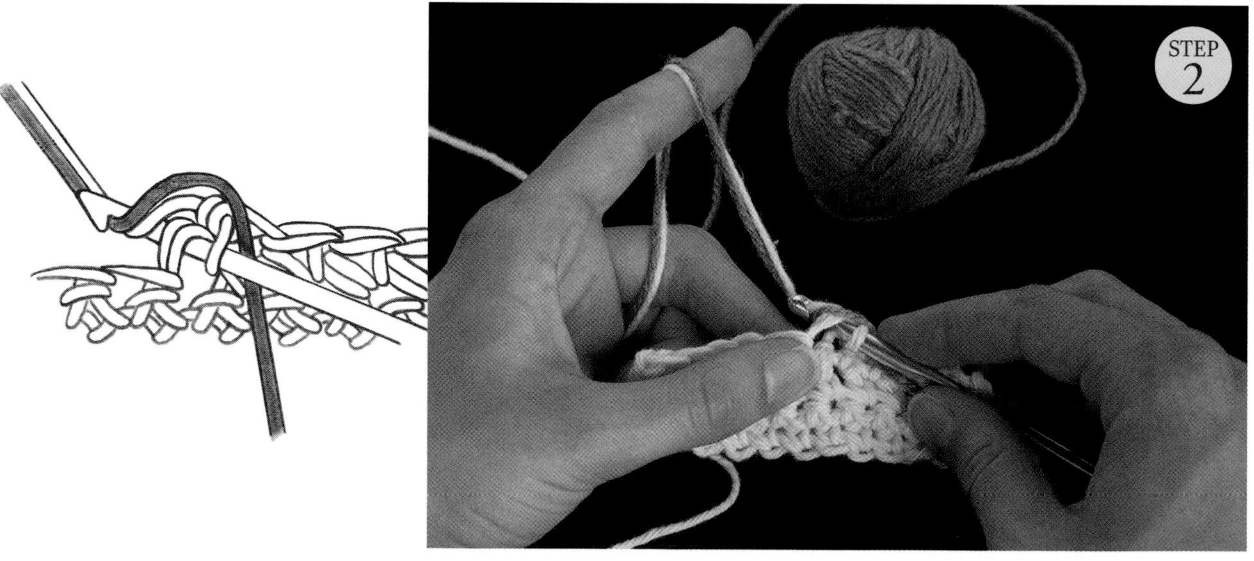

4. Work your stitches with the new yarn just like normal for the rest of the row. When your project is done, go back to the place where you started a new ball of yarn and thread the loose ends onto a blunt-tip needle. Feed the loose ends through several stitches to hold in place so nothing comes unraveled.

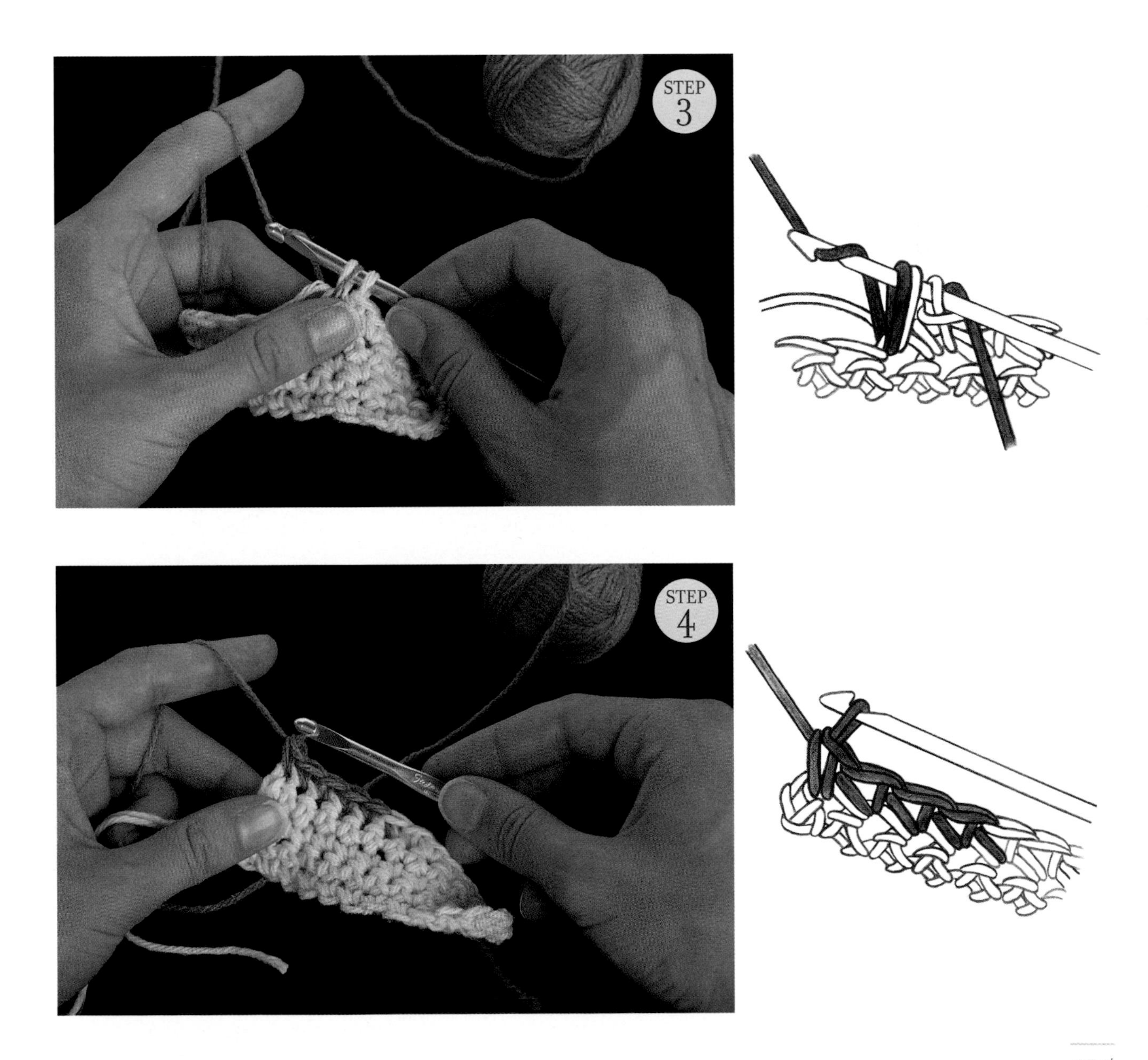

Working a Trellis Stitch

A trellis is simply a network of lengths of chains looped together to make a meshlike pattern when the weight of the fabric pulls down on it. This stitch must be used in a project where the number of stitches in each row is evenly divisible by four.

At the end of a row (our photos show a trellis worked into a row of double crochet), chain five stitches. Skip over three of the stitches from the previous row. Work one single crochet into the next stitch. Repeat that pattern all the way across the row. At the end of the row, turn your work around and get ready for the second row. For the second row, chain five stitches. Make one single crochet into the first five-chain space near the center (this means that your stitch goes all the way around the chain, not through one of the chains). Repeat this pattern all the way across the row and for all rows after this one.

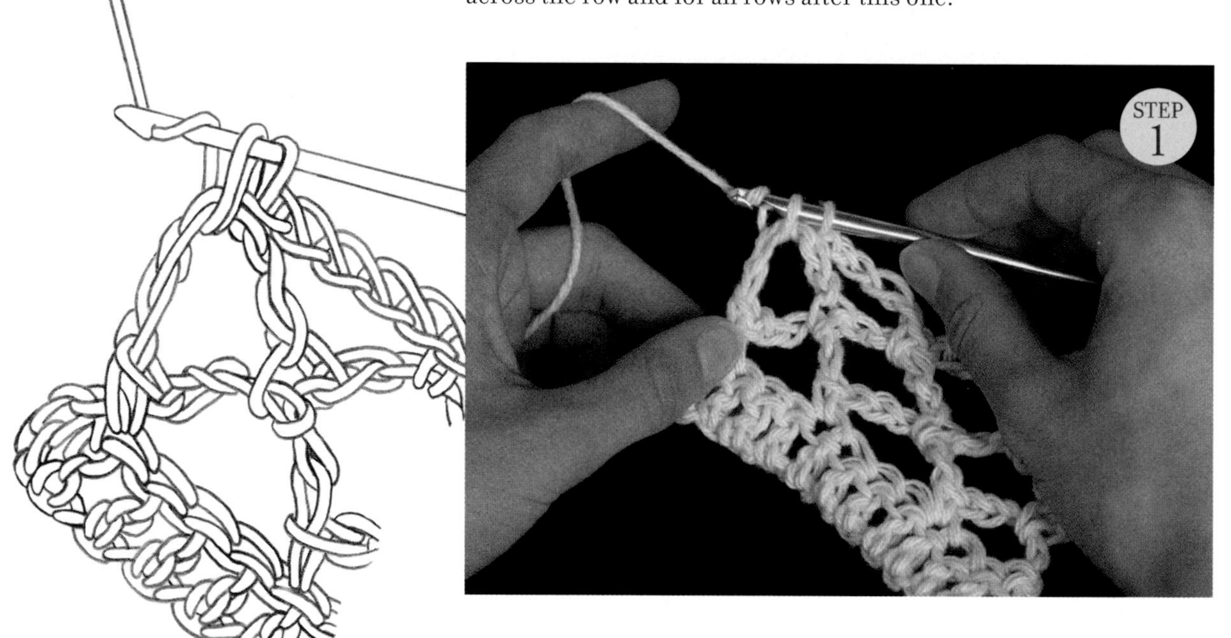

Working a Picot

A picot is simply a little loop of chains worked into one stitch to create a small "bubble" of crochet. It is often used to edge a finished piece for a decorative look.

1. All you have to do is slip stitch into a stitch and make three or four chains (your pattern should tell you exactly how many).
2. Slip stitch back into the same stitch.
3. Keep slip stitching through each stitch until it's time for another picot.

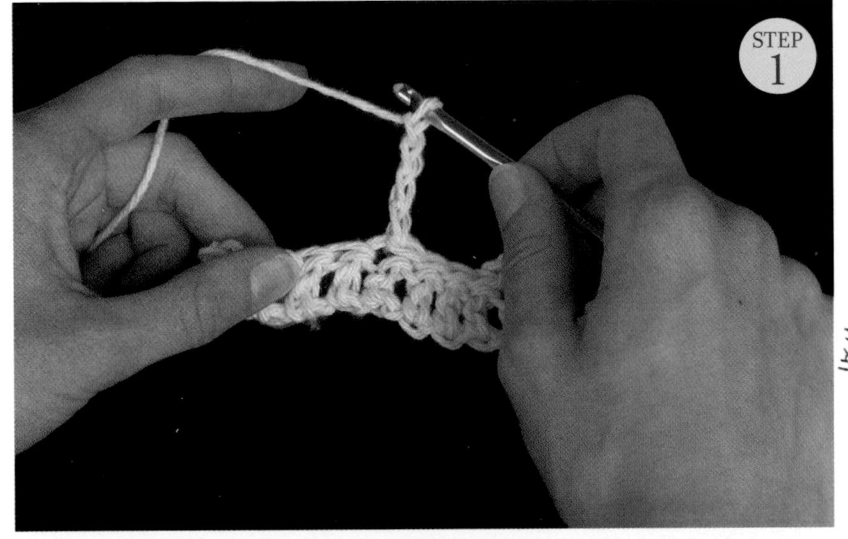
STEP
1

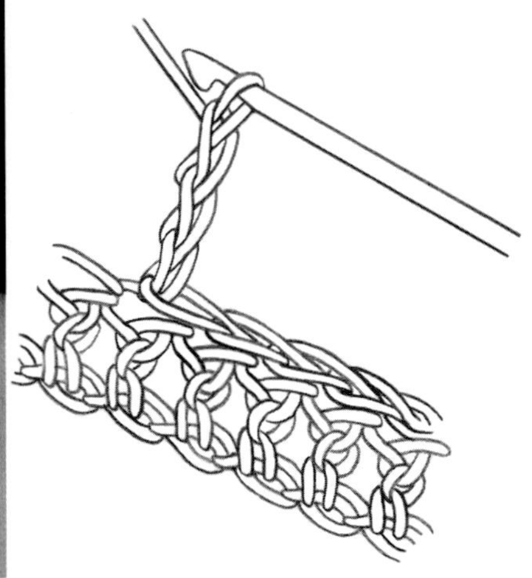

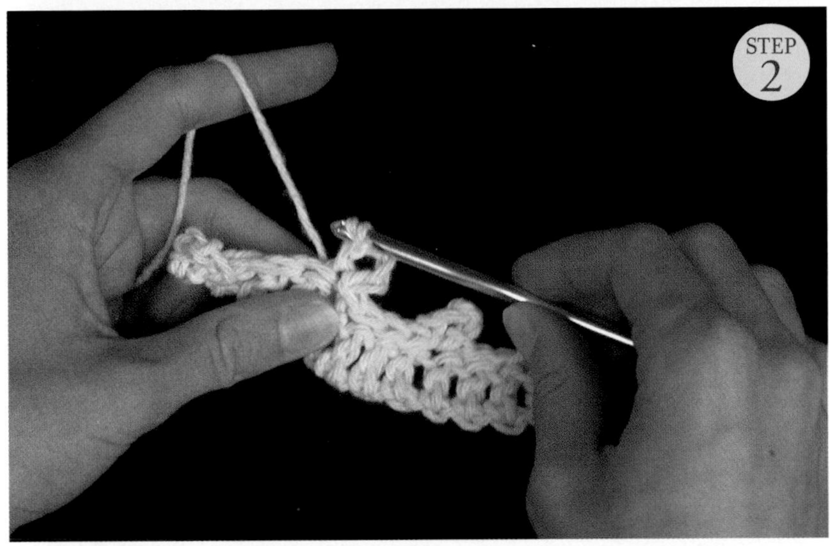
STEP
2

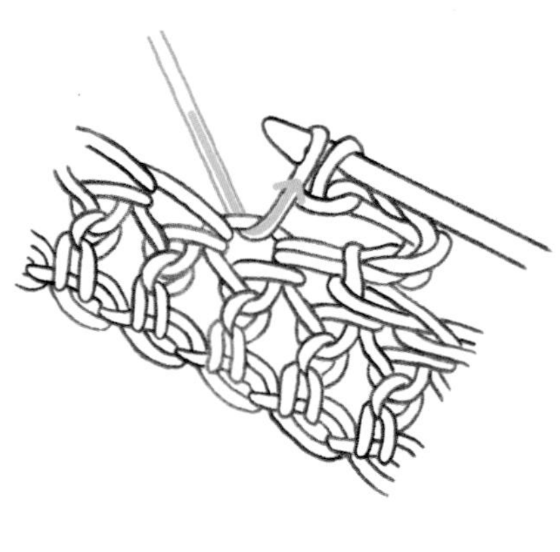

STEP
3

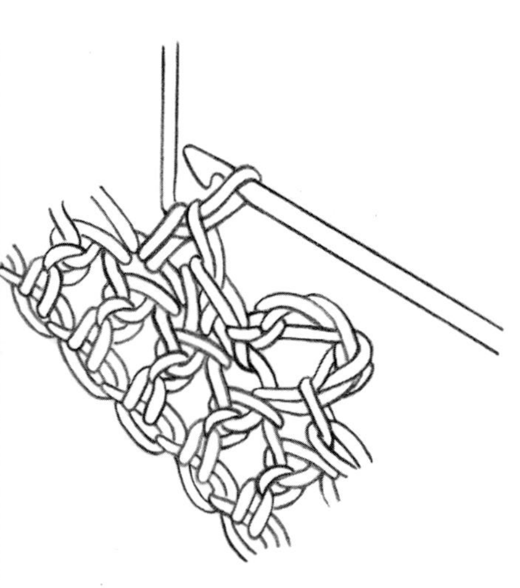

Fastening Off

Fastening off is the term for ending your work.

1. Cut your yarn, leaving a tail of 4–5" or so. Draw the loose end of your yarn through the loop on your hook and pull to tighten.
2. Weave in the loose end of yarn by threading it through a blunt-tip needle and weaving it through several stitches.

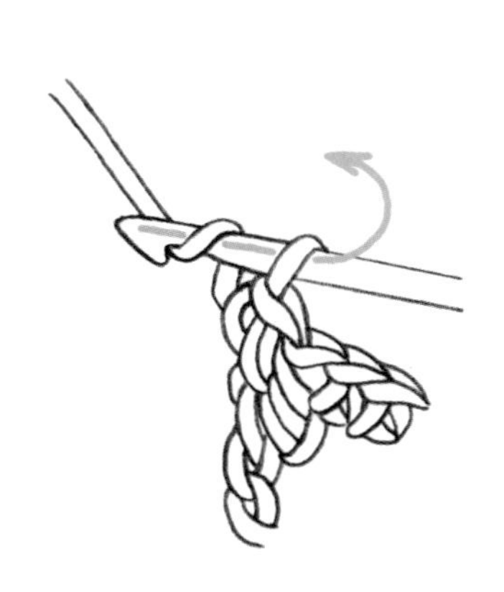

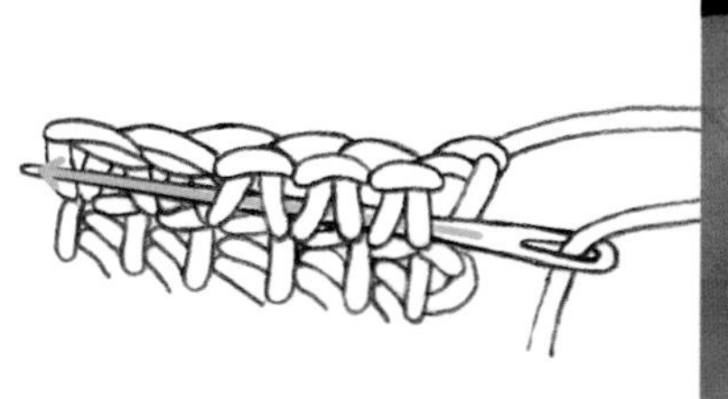

Attaching Two Pieces Together

1. This is just like sewing two pieces of fabric together. Match up the edges you want to attach with the right sides of the crochet together. Starting with a slip knot on your hook, work a slip stitch through the tops of the first stitches of both pieces of crochet.
2. Work a slip stitch into the tops of the rest of the stitches in the same manner. Remember, you always want to push your hook through both pieces of crochet, not just one or the other.

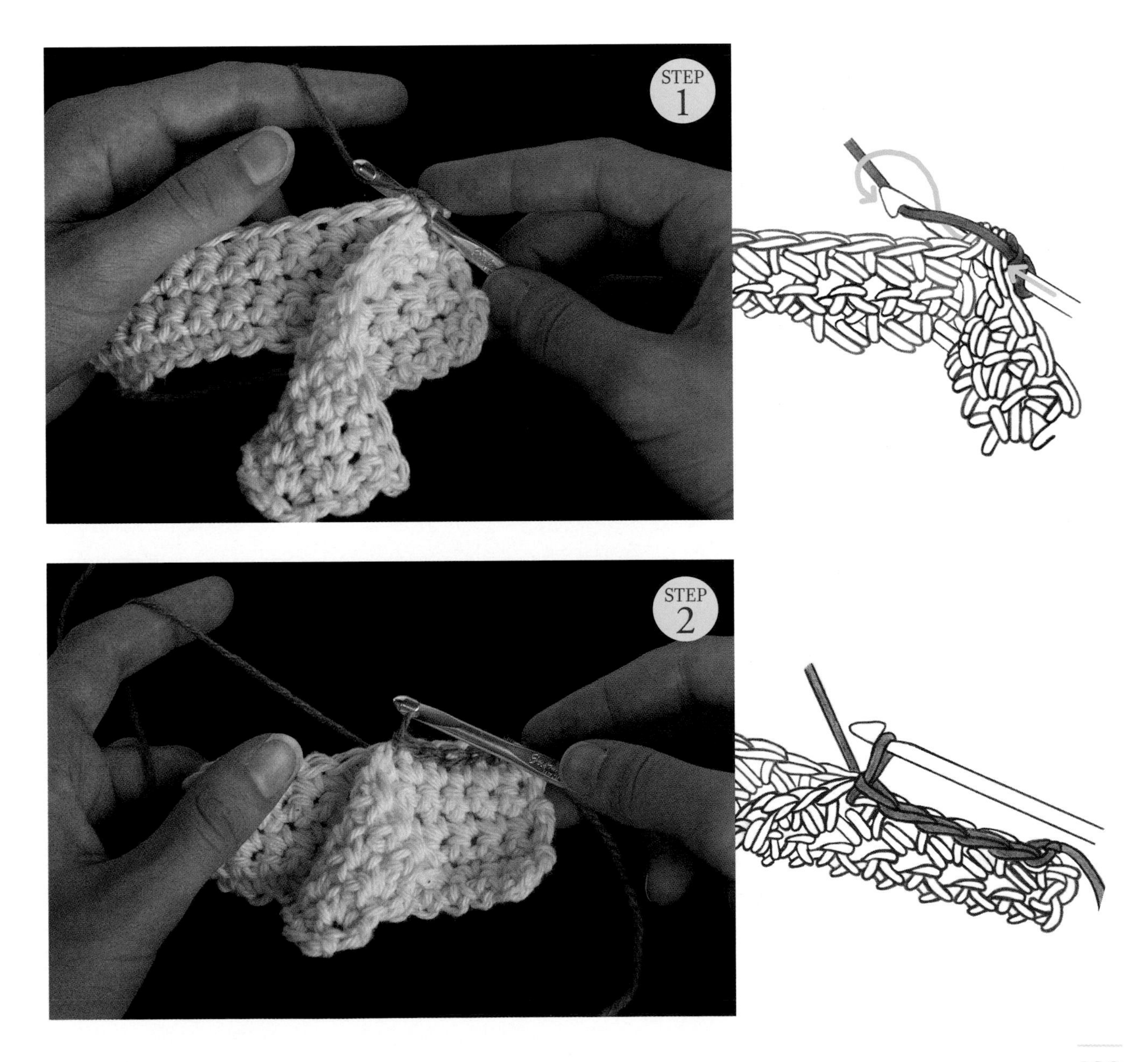

My mother wearing a double-tatted collar.

My daughter, Meggie, wearing a tatted collar embellished with French knots embroidered along the shoulders.

This book was just one big farmgirl stitchfest. Thanks to Anna Black (who never balked at any project or curve ball pitched her way); Julie Beck (who also helped run my bed-and-breakfast)—without her organizational nature, I couldn't have made it to this page; Andrea Atwood—her willingness to show up and pitch in with whatever was needed at the moment (as a single mother with seven children, I'm not sure how she even showed up at the farm, but she did); Barbara Peringer—a farmer's wife and rural mail carrier who worked from her home double-checking our patterns and making some of the aprons we sell (we cherish her valuable feedback, but more important, we *love* her rural savvy and steady calm); Dory Straight, Debbie Lewis, and Lynn Drivdahl, who created and checked patterns; Katy King and Katie Saunders, for their tatting expertise and lend-a-hand attitude; Jennifer Whitney, for her attention to detail while double-checking our patterns and instructions; Wendy Harbaugh and Carma Potter, for putting yet another eye to our patterns and instructions (Carma, a former local farmer who sold me the hundreds of irises that line my driveway, tackled my mother's hexagonal crochet patterns single-handedly); and Taylor Barrett, our former design assistant, for creating our dishtowel patterns before getting married and moving to Montana to start a family (we miss you, Taylor!). But my biggest stitchfelt thank you goes to Carol's friend, Teena Bechard. Teena came onto the scene almost after the fact, but I thank my lucky stars for her keen eye and formal training in pattern design. (Somebody had to do it: clean up after all of us!)

Gabe Gibler, my in-house illustrator (not by clear intention or design), came here four years ago as a volunteer with what I call a bookkeeper personality—an eye for detail. After mixing food for years, he became our bookkeeper and computer sharpshooter. That's when I started noticing little sketches everywhere. Gabe lent his talents to our crochet pages by drawing our how-to illustrations.

I'd like to thank the Latah County Historical Society and the McConnell Mansion for letting us use their museum for photography. Their efforts and accomplishments to preserve our past are priceless.

But the task of organizing and putting on paper everything I dream up is the hardest task of all. For editing, I'd like to thank Pam Krauss, Carol Hill, Will Pitkin, and Priscilla Wegars.

And about Carol Hill, my graphics designer and best friend—

what can I say? When Carol had a health crisis (the retina in her eye detached after she smacked it on the handle of a skillet while bending over to clean), I rushed her to surgery two hours away, praying with all my heart. I just couldn't or wouldn't want to do any of this without her farmgirl genius, her creativity, and her attention to detail. But most of all, I love how her laughter, her stick-to-it-iveness, and her poise motivate me to pursue my dreams full speed ahead.

Erik Jacobson, photographer and videographer, has become a miracle in my life. He really is a creative genius, though I hesitate to say that out loud, lest he get an offer to move elsewhere. And he's been such a great pal to Carol and me—the perfect esprit de corps fit. When he and Carol pick up their ukuleles and sing, "O gimme a moon, a prairie moon, and gimme a gal what's true, and let me wahoo, wahoo, wahoo!" I'm good for another round of how-to, make-do, why-for, will-do, and finger-pickin' can-do.

My husband, Nick Ogle, has to be the sweetest and most supportive husband on earth. And my kids, Meggie and Emil? Well, Meggie and her wonderful husband, Luke, have moved back home to farm full-time with me—every rural mother's dream come true. They bring with them an adorable little somebody who turned me into a "Nanny Jane." (Farmhand Amylou Johnson knitted our new little one the most precious comforter I've ever seen.) And Emil, along with his darling wife, Kate, left home so Emil can pursue a degree in diesel mechanics with an emphasis on biofuel. I miss them terribly! Both Meggie and Kate also helped stitch and model. What a blessing my children and their spouses are in my life!

Can you tell by now that I think I am just one lucky woman?

Oh, and thanks to the women on my chatroom who give me so many good ideas. To sign up for some fabulous farmgirl conversation, join the Farmgirl Connection at www.maryjanesfarm.org. Or better yet, sign up to start a farmgirl chapter in your own hometown, joining the thousands who gather together in true-blue farmgirl fashion for everything from barn raisings to community fundraisin', "sewie" swaps to hog-feeder talk, and tatting to mere chatting.

My most grateful thanks (as in grace before a meal) extends to everyone who buys my books and organic food, etc.!! We really do survive because of your generosity. At the end of every hardworking day, my husband calls out a tally of everything sold. We hope to stitch the world into a healthier place, one book at a time.

My maternal great-grandmother wearing both a handmade lace shawl and a crocheted collar.

My hair is held up in a crocheted head wrap. I'm wearing a bolero made from black netting gathered into yo-yos, netted together with crocheted trellis stitches.

Okay. You've gone through my book and earmarked all the projects you intend to stitch yourself, but your excitement doesn't allow you to wait another minute to start decorating your home (and yourself!) in lacy tattings, elegant cutwork, vintage lacework, ornamental yo-yos, and more. Eventually, for your own sanity, you'll want to make friends with a crochet needle or embroidery hoop (trust me on this), but until then it's time for some whimsy. Hit the flea markets and antiques shops to gussy up your walls, pillows, picture frames, windows, pockets, purses, coats, hats, towels, even socks ... it's endless, really. If you can't find or afford to buy perfect vintage pieces, don't turn away from a well-used or damaged piece of lace. Simply stitch it onto a pillow, purse, or scarf, or take a digital photo of its good corner and send it to www.simplycanvas.com. They specialize in enlarging images and printing them on canvas. Perfect for your office wall or that empty space above your bed! I remember my friend Cindylou saying she was going to spend the weekend stitching some of her grandmother's lace onto vintage fabric to make covers for her computer and printer. "I'm going to 'farmgirl up' my office," she said.

So, I hope our visit and time spent together in my Stitching Room has given you plenty of ideas for "farmgirlin' up" your own life!

INDEX

I N D E X

MaryJane & daughter Meggie

MaryJane Butters, a woman of many aprons, discovered she was a writer when she needed a mail-order catalog for the line of organic foods she produced at her Idaho farm. When her passion for good stories got out of hand, her catalog became a "storefront" magazine known as *MaryJanesFarm,* which found its way into stores like Barnes & Noble, Borders, and Wal-Mart, and eventually landed on the desk of a literary agent in New York.

MaryJane grew up in Utah in a self-sufficient family of seven, longing for fertile ground where she could raise her own flock of chickens, maybe a cow or two, and a family. Working her way north, she made her living as a carpenter, waitress, seamstress, secretary, janitor, wilderness ranger, community organizer, and milkmaid.

Rooted now on her own five acres for the past twenty-one years (seven of those as a single mom), MaryJane, at fifty-three, has accomplished everything she set out to achieve, including a few surprises. Fourteen years ago she married her neighbor, Nick Ogle, a third-generation farmer. Together they raised four hardworking children, plus bees, chickens, goats, cows, peas, beans, hay, wheat, and every vegetable imaginable, including a biodiesel crop to fuel MaryJane's car. She has cultivated organic farmers for eleven years in her apprenticeship program called Pay Dirt Farm School, launched Project F.A.R.M. (First-class American Rural Made), bought a historic flour mill, and created the Farmgirl Connection, a website that brings together thousands of women to share their farmgirl dreams and big farmgirl hearts, www.maryjanesfarm.org/farmgirl-connection.